Spiritual Direction in the
Dominican Tradition

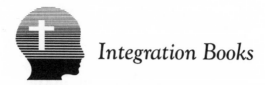

Integration Books

STUDIES IN PASTORAL PSYCHOLOGY,
THEOLOGY, AND SPIRITUALITY
ROBERT J. WICKS, GENERAL EDITOR

also in the series

Spiritual Direction in the Dominican Tradition

Benedict M. Ashley, O.P.

Integration Books

paulist press / new york / mahwah

Cover design by James F. Brisson.

Cover photo credit: Kenneth C. Perry, ST. DOMINIC by Thomas M. McGlynn, Bronze, 6'-4", located on Providence College Campus, 1st casting: Madonna del Arco, Naples.

Library of Congress Cataloging-in-Publication Data

Ashley, Benedict M.
   Spiritual direction in the Dominican tradition / Benedict M. Ashley.
     p. cm. — (Integration books)
   Includes bibliographical references and index.
   ISBN 0-8091-3567-1 (alk. paper)
   1. Dominicans—Spiritual life. 2. Spiritual direction.
I. Title. II. Series.
BX3503.A74 1995   94-46496
255'.2—dc20   CIP

Published by Paulist Press
997 Macarthur Boulevard
Mahwah, NJ 07430

Printed and bound in the
United States of America

Contents

*To My Brethren
of St. Louis Bertrand Priory,
St. Louis,
for Their Fraternal Love
and Spiritual Direction*

Acknowledgments

A theme of this book is that in the Dominican tradition spiritual direction for a member of the Dominican Order comes principally from living in a Christian community. It is the mutual help, good example, striving for holiness, common mission and collaboration, and stimulating diversity and constructive conflict of community living that best enable us to draw closer to Christ.

Consequently, I warmly thank my Dominican brothers and sisters for such living truth as I have been able to express in this book. First of all I want to thank Michael A. Ciccone, O.P., for suggesting me for this project to the series editor Robert Wicks, to Romanus Cessario, O.P., for his friendship and encouragement, and to the Dominican Priory of the Immaculate Conception, Washington, D.C., and its then prior John A. Farren, O.P. who gave me such gracious hospitality as I began the book. Especial thanks is due Donald Goergen, O.P., former provincial of my home province of St. Albert the Great, and to my brothers of Priory of St. Louis Bertrand, St. Louis, with whom I now reside and to whom I dedicate this book and to Aquinas Institute of Theology of which I am a professor emeritus.

I also sincerely thank Carl Anderson, Dean of the Institute for Studies and Marriage and Family, Washington, D.C., where I formerly taught and my graduate assistant at the Institute, Gloria Dodd. In my study of the tradition of Dominican spirituality I have been greatly inspired and assisted by William Hinnebusch, O.P., now deceased, by Sister Mary Nona McGreal, O.P., and by Parable, a collaborative enterprise of women and men Dominicans.

Foreword

With a beautiful grasp of the Dominican tradition, Benedict Ashley, O.P., gives us a rich historical overview of the major personalities who contributed to this school of spirituality. In a concise, informative manuscript he traces the development of the tradition and presents the central elements that form and guide a Dominican spiritual director.

In this tightly written book we are introduced to writers and mentors upon whom we can focus further should we wish (ample notes and bibliography are provided). We are also given a sense of the controversies and anthropology that shaped much of the tradition in spirituality we refer to as "Dominican."

In the spirit of Thomas Aquinas, Benedict Ashley helps us see that spiritual counselors must "go deeper and raise the questions about whether the persons who seek their guidance are *really* committed to the goals, to which they claim to be committed, or whether there is something false and hypocritical about this commitment. Or, to look at it from the client's point of view, we go to a spiritual director because we want to be a good person, but we realize that somehow in our hearts we are resisting a full and genuine commitment to God and our true self, and we need to be delivered from these resistances. Thus the spiritual director's questions must always seek to help the client penetrate these delusions, this pride, and false claims to absolute autonomy, and to open up to God's grace."

He also helps us to see how fundamental grace, God's generous love, is to the process of living a full spiritual life. With classic Dominican optimism, Ashley emphasizes that even sin cannot deprive us of God's constant desire for us to share in divine love.

In the chapter specifically dealing with ministry, the need for, and the goals of spiritual direction and the guidelines of being a good direc-

1

tor are addressed. This area in other books often tends to be very anecdotal in nature. However, here he remains faithful to the task of the book by offering content, quotes, and reflections by classic and more contemporary Dominican writers.

Finally, the "three processes of spiritual growth" are addressed. This closing section, comprised of three chapters on purification, illumination, and union with God, is scholarly, practical, clear, and—in the spirit of Dominic—both very human and simple in nature. In this material he examines these three "stairs" to encounter with God and offers them as a structure for understanding one's own spiritual journey as well as counseling others interested in the quest to embrace the living God fully in daily life.

Having a book like this on direction which allows us to have companions such as Dominic, Aquinas, Eckhart, Vincent Ferrer, Catherine de Ricci, Philip Neri, Henry Suso and others as we examine the spiritual life is a real joy. I think persons interested in the process of spiritual direction and interested in the tapestry of ideas and suggestions of persons in the Dominican tradition will find Benedict Ashley's book a small treasure house of information.

Robert J. Wicks
Series Editor

Chapter 1

The Development of the Tradition

One Among Many

The tradition of spirituality proper to the Order of Preachers, and of the whole Dominican family of nuns, sisters, and laity founded by St. Dominic de Guzman is only one of the many such traditions that have been historically important in Christianity and which also remain influential today. In this book I claim no more for it than that, even when—because it has been my own vocation and my life—I may seem to boast of its superiority to all others. I present it here in hopes that some of its riches may prove useful not only to those of my tradition but also to those to whom it is unfamiliar.

In chapter 1, I will sketch the historical development of this tradition, emphasizing certain theological controversies that have shaped it. In chapter 2, I will analyze the structure and dynamics of the human person who needs to grow spiritually. In chapter 3, I will inquire how the grace of Christ working through his Holy Spirit transforms nature in this process of spiritual growth. In chapter 4, I will ask what role a director plays in this process of transformation. Finally in chapters 5, 6, and 7, I will look at the processes of purification, illumination, and union which bring about this growth and transformation and which a spiritual director seeks to promote.

Dominic's Way

St. Dominic, who was to create a new form of Christian spirituality in the church, was born, in Caleruega, Spain, between 1171 and 1173, one of the three sons of a local overlord, Felix de Guzman and of Jane of Aza, a noblewoman remembered for her sanctity. Educated first by his uncle, a priest, and then at a school which was soon to become the

University of Palencia, he became a canon under the reforming bishop of Osma, Diego de Azvedo, and soon sub-prior of the cathedral chapter. After a diplomatic visit with his bishop to Denmark in 1203, he traveled to southern France, where he came in contact with Albigensian or Manichaean heretics, who attributed the creation of the world to an evil God. He was deeply troubled by the people's ignorance of the gospel, which made them so vulnerable to this revival of ancient Gnosticism.

After returning to Spain the bishop and Dominic had to make a second visit to Denmark. On their return they visited Rome and begged Pope Innocent III to send them on the missions, but the pope said the bishop was needed at home. Dominic, however, remained in southern France and began life as a traveling preacher, along with a group of Cistercian abbots, continuing the mission after they had departed. After nine years of such preaching on his own, in 1215 he accompanied the Bishop of Toulouse to Rome, and in 1216 obtained permission to found an Order of Preachers dedicated exclusively to "preaching and the salvation of souls."

Dominic began his community in Toulouse with some sixteen brothers whom he had gathered during the course of his preaching. Almost immediately he dispersed them to spread the mission and then himself traveled throughout Spain and northern Italy to found new priories. In 1220 the first General Chapter of the Order was held at which Dominic sought, but was not permitted by his friars, to resign as Master of the Order. At a second chapter in 1221 the *Constitutions* of the order took final form under his guidance. Dominic hoped then to go on the missions to eastern Europe which had always been his desire, but he died in Bologna, August 6, 1221. He was canonized in 1234 by Gregory IX, who as cardinal had aided both him and St. Francis in obtaining papal approval of their respective orders.

The memory of Dominic's personality was perhaps best captured by the mystic Dominican-directed Mechtilde of Magdeburg (d. 1297) who said of him,[1]

St. Dominic taught the wise that they should temper their knowledge with divine simplicity; to the simple he taught true wisdom; the tempted he helped to bear their sorrows secretly. He taught the young to keep much silence that they might be outwardly modest and inwardly wise. The sick and infirm he comforted with true compassion, caring for all their needs. They rejoiced at the long years he spent among them; his gracious company made their labors light....God has specially honored his two sons, Francis and Dominic, with four things:...to welcome all; to give real help in every need; to possess the holy wisdom of Divine Truth; and cherish the power of his Holy Church.

From the *Acts of Canonization*, one gets the impression that Dominic had the graciousness of which Humbert of Romans, in his classic *Treatise on Preaching*, wrote,[2]

Finally, since all of these will be of little value unless there is a graciousness upon the lips, in accordance with what it says in Sirach 20:21, "A man without grace is like an idle tale," above everything else it is necessary for a preacher to have grace in his speaking, grace to season everything. This is what is said of the best preacher of all in Psalm 44:3, "Grace is poured upon your lips."

St. Francis and St. Dominic were original in creating communities not of monks but of brethren (friars). Monasticism (from *monos*, a solitary) had grown out of the contemplative life of the hermits of the desert, and was organized on the basis of commitment to a local monastery headed by an abbot (spiritual father). These new mendicant orders differed markedly from monasticism in that they were sustained not by the ownership and cultivation of lands, but by begging; were international rather than local in membership; and lived democratically as brotherhoods with elected officials, rather than under the monarchy of a spiritual father.

Both Dominic and Francis aimed at reviving the wandering "apostolic life" in total poverty of the first disciples of Jesus, but their two orders differed in that Francis sought simply to give an example of Christian living, and originally drew his friars from the laity, while Dominic had the specific aim of preaching, and therefore founded an order of priests under the canonical *Rule of St. Augustine* (under which he had begun his own priestly life as a canon) to assist the bishops in their teaching office, although he included non-ordained members: co-operator brothers to assist in this mission, and contemplative nuns to empower it through prayer. Later this Dominican family was also to include laypeople.

For Dominic, the work of preaching the word of God came first and, as the *Constitutions* written under his direction show, it was this mission which shaped every aspect of his spirituality and his community. He insisted that these rules could be modified by the chapters and dispensed by the provincials and priors in favor of the needs of the missions. Evidently he felt that the spiritual formation and direction of Dominicans should come primarily, not from a spiritual father, but from living in a community inspired by the very mission that Jesus had chosen for himself, the ministry of the word.

This ministry of the word was a specific one—to communicate the message of the gospel in a way that would penetrate the mind and hearts of people as a "two-edged sword" (Heb 4:12). It was to fulfill the Pauline injunction (2 Tm 4:2–5):

> Proclaim the word; be persistent whether it is convenient or inconvenient; convince, reprimand, encourage through all patience and teaching. For the time will come when people will not tolerate sound doctrine but, following their own desires and insatiable curiosity, will accumulate teachers and will stop listening to the truth and will be diverted to myths. But you, be self-possessed in all circumstances; put up with hardship; perform the work of an evangelist, fulfill your ministry.

This ministry was to extend to all, from the lowliest and least educated to the cultured and intellectual, and it was not confined to any place or time, nor to any particular medium. Dominic himself, however, carried it on by the living voice (he left us no writings) and not merely in church but in all kinds of public places.

The eyewitness testimonies at Dominic's canonization show that Dominic had no intention of acting the role of an abbot or spiritual guide, although he was the leader of his preachers and was noted for the kindly and encouraging way he dealt with them, and for his own example of courage and cheerfulness in meeting the difficulties of an apostle's life and work. Dominican communities are headed by a prior (number one brother) elected for a term by the brethren, who leads with the assistance of the chapter of the brethren. These priories are organized into provinces elected by the priories, under a prior provincial and a provincial chapter, and the provinces by a Master of the Order and a general chapter. Thus community life and government have a fundamentally democratic, participatory character.

Although Dominic made the mission primary, he was profoundly convinced that preaching is a work of grace, not of human eloquence, and consequently must receive its power from prayer. This is shown by the fact that even before he gathered his friars, he first founded a community of cloistered, contemplative nuns at Prouille in France, and while still getting his order under way, hastened to found communities of contemplative women at Madrid and Rome. Hence, unlike the later St. Ignatius Loyola who, for the sake of mission, eliminated monastic practices, Dominic retained many of them—the liturgy of the hours and community eucharist, the cloister and silence, fasting and other penances. He himself was given to constant prayer, and a beautiful little anonymous work *The Nine Ways of Prayer* has preserved for us his ways of praying with his whole body, heart and mind.[3] He was also given to long night vigils and to severe physical penances, scourging himself to blood, while groaning deeply in compassion for those to whom he preached, since, as he said, he wished that he might throw his body over the mouth of hell to close it to sinners.

What was unusual, however, was that St. Dominic did not see prayer and penance alone as sufficient to prepare his preachers. The ancient monks had prayed and labored, and had also studied the scriptures (*lectio divina*) as a help to meditation. Dominic went further. From the very beginning he sent some of his friars to study at the University of Paris, because he was convinced that for the range of preaching required of the bishops whom his preachers were to assist, not only the simple exhortations which St. Francis commended to his friars, but also profound theological preaching was necessary. Nothing less could meet the attacks of the often learned heretics whom he had met among the Manichees. Every priory, therefore, was to have at least one well-trained teacher (the lector) who could teach the other friars, and soon houses of study (*studia*) were founded, many integrated into the great universities of the day.

Thus we can sum up the basic principles of the spirituality of St. Dominic's order as: (1) to follow the Lord Jesus in the ministry of the word; (2) not as mere individuals, but as a band of preachers like the twelve apostles, supporting one another in the mission; (3) so as to preach not worldly wisdom but the incarnate Word whom they had come to know through deep liturgical and personal prayer; and (4) enlightened by constant study of the word of God and of all learning necessary to make it credible to people of all classes, places, and times.[4]

To trace the development of this original spirituality, rather than proceed strictly chronologically, I will group the important figures according to certain main tendencies.

Humbert of Romans and Dominican Formation

In the thirteenth century the spirituality of the order and the way it was transmitted from one generation to the next took concrete shape. The central figure in this tradition of religious formation was the fifth Master of the Order, Humbert of Romans (1252–1263, d. 1277) who left us commentaries and treatises *On the Rule, On the Constitutions, On the Offices of the Order, On the Work of Preaching, On Preaching the Crusade* and a lengthy work for the Council of Lyons on the missions and the reform of the church, besides encyclical letters to the order on obedience, regular observance, chastity, humility, and patience in suffering. Often attributed to him is another thirteenth work on the training of novices whose true author is unknown.[5]

These treatises show us that the masters of novices were expected to instruct their charges in the basic features of Dominican life, and the priors were to continue this for the professed members. Of great importance was the "Chapter of Faults" at which each friar confessed his breaches of the rule and reported to the whole community infractions by others. The prior admonished the offender, assigned a penance, and urged forgiveness and reconciliation. The emphasis was on the observance of the required fasts (which were rather severe) and of the prescribed periods of silence, prompt attendance at the liturgy, cheerful fulfillment of assigned duties, charity in conversation and in relation to others, humility in receiving corrections and in their studies, and readiness to forgive offenses. The type of spirituality then most influential on Dominicans is indicated by the writers Humbert recommends to the novices: John Cassian, Hugh of St. Victor, Bernard of Clairvaux, William of St. Thierry, and the Dominican, Guillaume de Peyraut.

Gerard of Frachet (d. 1271) who, at the request of Humbert, had collected the memories of the first friars in *The Lives of the Brethren* (1268) gives this picture of the Order's "first fervor."[6]

Who shall tell of their devotion to the blessed Virgin!...After Matins and Compline they girt her altar in a triple row, kneeling thus they fervently commended themselves and the Order to her protection. They had her image and her Son's in their cells, so that whether reading or praying, or sleeping, they might cast loving glances upon them....They exchanged mutual kind deeds in the infirmary, hospice, or at table, even stooping to wash each other's feet, and deeming him happiest who forestalled the others in such charitable offices....Such joy and fervor beamed on their faces as they waited on each other, that they seemed to be serving God and his angels instead of men....In pursuit of their apostolic ministry for which the Order had been intended from the beginning, God poured out upon them such marvelous zeal and fervor that many could not eat without qualms of conscience unless they had preached that day to many or to a few, and in this matter the Holy Spirit made good, by inward unction, whatever was wanting to them of acquired knowledge. They often drew many to conversion by the simple text of the seven canonical hours, which, together with St. Matthew's Gospel, St. Dominic used frequently to expound to them.

Yet we need to set against this idealization of the first days of the order the lament of Humbert of Romans, the fifth Master of the Order, in an encyclical letter following the chapter of 1261 held in Barcelona. After expressing his joy in the reports of many good works by the friars which he had received, he goes on:[7]

From the reports, there has not ceased a splendor in buildings, elaboration in dress, curiosity [rather than serious study] in their work, superfluity in their meals and disputes among some of them in their goings on which causes no little scandal in the world. Moreover, it was brought out that novices are badly formed, and even before their due time the less suitable are dangerously exposed; useless discourses are not quelled, nor are those corrected who violate the customs of the Order in their manner of travel. Many are frequently involved in secular and transitory matters and many scandalize the Order by their indolence....Many indeed are careless about keeping peace with the secular clergy. Several bold ones act without permission. Many are willing to attempt things of which they are ignorant, yet unwilling to do what displeases them. They are careless in their behavior, pernicious in their example. How foolishly they go among those outside the Order, how lightly they discard the fasts, how much they neglect the study of sacred doctrine! How idly they pass their time, how little they devote to the examination of conscience, to the perfecting of unity, to the harmony of life, to control of the tongue, to the discipline of the senses—and to many other matters which so many chapters, so many Fathers of the Order, so often, with great deliberation, continue to decree! These are matters, dearly beloved, by which the Chapters are defrauded of their annual harvest, which cause tried brethren laboring for the Order to weep, since their heavy labors seem to have been in vain.

Thus, from an early period there has been no lack of realistic self-criticism among Dominicans concerning their failures to match their ideals. Yet this has not prevented the transmission of the values for which Dominic founded his order. How these values were communicated in the thirteenth century is made clear by the books for preachers written during this period, such as the *Summa of Virtues and Vices* (1248) of Guillaume Peyraut (23 editions from 1500–1668) and the collections of stories for sermons (*exempla*) of Étienne de Bourbon, by the encyclopedia for preachers of Vincent of Beauvais, the biblical commentaries of Hugh of St. Cher, and the sermons and book of *exempla* of Giovanni de San Gimignano (d. 1337).

The Dominican liturgy was soon standardized, largely based on that of the Cistercians, but made uniform so that preachers traveling about would be familiar with common practices. The Roman rite was followed along with a selection of local customs, and with a simplification of the chant so as to keep the liturgy relatively brief; but the hours, including the night office were sung at the appropriate times not, as they often later were, jammed together or "anticipated." Following St. Dominic's love of prayer with bodily gestures, the Dominican office was noted for its processions, various kinds of bows, genuflections, and prostrations.

Nevertheless, in an order where study was emphasized, it was to be expected that this simple but expressive prayer life would also be controlled by theological speculation. The fundamental figures in this regard in the order's first century were St. Albert the Great, and his brilliant pupil St. Thomas Aquinas, but there were others, such as Bl. Peter of Tarantaise (the future Pope Innocent V), and the great canonist St. Raymund of Peñafort. It was Albert, Thomas, and Peter who designed the intellectual formation *(ratio studiorum)* for the order, in which theological studies were to be preceded by study of the liberal arts and philosophy. This gave to the order a scholarly cast that stimulated many members to seek academic degrees and to become teachers, both to the advantage of preaching and sometimes to its disadvantage, because academic ambition often tended to suppress apostolic zeal.

From Albert the Great stemmed two very different ways of understanding theology and the spiritual life. One was that of St. Thomas Aquinas, with its emphasis on an Aristotelian objective intellectuality, the other, developing in the next century, of Meister Eckhart, with its emphasis on a Platonic mysticism.

The Thomistic Tradition

Neither St. Albert the Great nor St. Thomas Aquinas separated spirituality from the context of a total developmental view of the Christian life and the virtues required to meet life's various problems and opportunities. Aquinas said, "We rather know what God is not than what he is." It is said that when, at the end of his life, a disciple asked him, "Master, why have you ceased to write?" he answered, "Compared with what has been revealed to me, all that I have written seems but straw." Clearly he was aware of the importance of apophatic or negative theology, but his own approach is essentially kataphatic or positive, seeking to rise from the analogy of the things we know from experience, to a positive (though purely analogical and wholly inadequate) notion of the Divine Mystery.

St. Thomas' masterwork, the *Summa Theologiae*, is an account of how humanity, made in the image of the Trinity, has come forth in creation from God, fallen into sin, yet has been called back to God through Jesus Christ. This is the final synthesis Aquinas made of his many other works of spiritual import, such as the earlier *Commentary on the Sentences*, the *Summa Contra Gentiles* written for missionaries to Islam, his commentaries on Job and the first fifty-four psalms, on the gospels of Matthew and John and the epistles of St. Paul, on the Creed, the Our Father and Hail Mary, and the Ten Commandments, his defense of the mendicant orders against the criticisms of the secular clergy, and so on. Since these writings were to become the main sources for the whole subsequent history of Dominican spirituality, their themes will be treated extensively in later chapters.

In the first quarter of the thirteenth century the theology and philosophy of Aquinas were adopted by the order as official, and all teachers and preachers were required by the General Chapters to conform to it, thus excluding the Nominalism which had come to dominate the universities and had influenced some Dominicans such as Durandus of Pourcain. Thomistic theologians such as Hervé de Nedellec and Peter de Palu engaged in controversies over the question of the poverty of Christ, striving to moderate the extreme views of the Franciscan "spirituals," to raise objections to the Franciscan teaching on the Immaculate Conception lest it detract from the universality of redemption through Christ, and to defend papal authority against the attacks of King Philip the Fair of France. It was not, however, until 1629 that Dominicans were required to adhere to the "solid doctrine" of St. Thomas by oath, a requirement removed after Vatican II.[8]

Negative and Bridal Mysticism

The priests of the order were originally reluctant to take responsibility for the spiritual direction of the nuns, but Humbert of Romans accepted this task for the order. It is exemplified in the letters of spiritual direction that had been written earlier by the second Master of the Order, Bl. Jordan of Saxony, to the nun Diana d'Andolò, foundress of the Dominican monastery in Bologna, and the letters and poems of Peter of Dacia to a mystic (not a Dominican) Christine of Stommeln and her circle. Mechtilde of Magdeburg, although not formally a Dominican, had Dominican spiritual directors both as a laywoman and after she entered in her old age the Cistercian nunnery of Helfta. There she influenced the important Cistercian mystics and spiritual writers St. Gertrude the Great and St. Mechtilde of Hackeborn. She left us in her own poetry and prose revelations, *The Flowing Light of the Godhead*, evidence of her devotion to St. Dominic. These give us an intimate view of the spirituality of the nuns of this century, based on a Bride of Christ mysticism. This group of contemplatives emphasized devotion to the Sacred Heart of Jesus as did Bl. Jutta de Sangerhausen (d.1260), also of Helfta, a widow and solitary.

Less is known about the inner life of St. Margaret of Hungary, but the eyewitnesses for her canonization tells how this royal princess chose for her own the most menial tasks of the community and of her personal care for the poor. The general impression that these first-hand sources convey is of spirituality which emphasizes an intimate personal relation to Christ shared in a simple, uncomplicated, affectionate way among brothers, sisters, and friends. Asceticism and patience in trials were heavily stressed, but the emotional life was warm and its verbal and gestural expression spontaneous.

After the first joyful, confident years of the order, it began to share in the anxieties of the fourteenth century, when Europe was devastated by the Black Death, the wars of rising national states, and the control of the papacy by the kings of France, resulting in three rival popes. No wonder that at this time the number of women in northern Europe entering the cloister vastly increased, and especially among the Dominican nuns there grew up what is called "Rhineland Mysticism" which has left us many spiritual autobiographies and biographies, such as the *Lives of the Sisters* by Catherine Geberschweir of Colmar, and the important writings of Bl. Margaret Ebner. This devotion centered on an intense personal relationship with Jesus in his passion. Some of these nuns were in correspondence with the Italian preacher, Venturino of Bergamo (d. 1346), whose letters of direction, On *Spiritual Perfection*, have also survived.[9]

Yet such mysticism had no systematic theory until Meister Eckhart of Erfurt and Cologne, a disciple, although not, like Thomas, an actual pupil of St. Albert the Great, put forth in commentaries, treatises, and sermons in Latin and in Middle High German a "mysticism of detachment" (*gelassenheit*) that was to influence the whole history of the church.

Eckhart had taught at the University of Paris, then at Cologne, and had become provincial of Saxony. Already in Germany the influence of Albert had stirred up much intellectual activity among Dominicans. John of Sterngassen (fl. 1325) was a noted German preacher and theologian; Gerard of Sterngassen (fl. 1335) had published *The Garden of Souls or a Remedy for the Troubled Soul* on the capital sins, the virtues, the gifts, and the beatitudes, and Nicholas of Strasbourg (fl. 1329) a defender of Eckhart wrote a *Summa philosophica*, and a work on the Second Coming of Christ. Hugh Ripelin of Strasbourg (d.c. 1270) wrote an Albertine *Compendium of Theological Truth*, which proved very popular and was later used by Suso and Tauler, important disciples of Eckhart. Hermann de Minden, the German provincial, who was concerned about heretical tendencies among the increasing number of Dominican nuns, in 1286 had established a policy of sending learned friars to give them spiritual direction. Hence, Eckhart himself, through this experience with contemplative nuns began to develop a remarkable mystical theology based on the ancient writings of the Pseudo-Dionysius profoundly colored by the Neoplatonic philosophy of the third-century pagan Plotinus.

The central theme of this apophatic or "negative" theology is that we cannot attain union with God except by becoming, as it were, a spiritual void, empty of all earthly thoughts and desires. This will make it possible for the eternal word of God to be born in the very depth of our souls, in that part of our self which is, as it were, a spark of the divine.[10] Eckhart, therefore, tried to lead the contemplatives he guided into this spiritual void or "night of faith" by the use of paradoxical sayings, somewhat like those *kohans* used by the Zen Buddhist masters, such as, "The eye by which I see God is the eye by which God sees me." Because these sayings, entirely orthodox in intention and often drawn from the gospel according to St. John, also were liable to a pantheistic interpretation, Eckhart was summoned to the papal court at Avignon to explain his teaching. He submitted to the guidance of the church and was never personally censured, but after his death (1328) some of these ambiguous sayings were condemned by the papal commission.

Although Eckhart's own writings were under a shadow, his followers gave them an orthodox interpretation. The most influential of these were Henry Suso (d. 1366) whose work *The Exemplar* was a collection of prose and poetry, and included a biography of Suso himself by a Dominican nun, Elisabeth Stagel, *The Life of the Servant*. One of Henry's most influential works was his *The Little Book of Eternal Wisdom*. His version of Eckhart's mysticism was much more centered than was his master's on the incarnate word and the passion and was poetically imaginative and affective.[11] John Tauler (d. 1361) had a whole circle of "Friends of God" which included the secular priest Henry of Nordlingen (d. 1351) who translated the works of Mechtilde of Magdeburg, and corresponded with Margaret Ebner and Venturino of Bergamo. Tauler's collected sermons, or *Conferences*, which very carefully warned against interpreting Eckhart in a *quietist* sense became immensely popular. On the other hand, Suso's works in translation traveled to Spain and laid the foundation of the spirituality of the great Spanish mystics such as Teresa of Avila and especially John of the Cross, with his doctrine of the "night of the soul" and "night of the spirit." Thus "negative theology" in the West always bears the mark of Eckhart.

The Catherinian and Prophetic Tradition

In Italy, however, the more positive Thomistic tradition flourished, as is evident in the many popular spiritual writings of Dominic Cavalca (d. 1342), notably his *The Mirror of the Cross*. Under the influence of Cavalca, a major Dominican figure, often considered the "Second Founder" of the Dominican Order, is St. Catherine of Siena (d. 1380). Catherine was not a nun, but a laywoman living the consecrated life, who gathered around herself a group of laity and clergy, including Raymund of Capua, her confessor and future Master of the Order.

Although Catherine was a mystic of the highest order and a stigmatic, her spirituality as expressed in her many letters of spiritual direction and her *Dialogue* centers not on inner experience but on the love of God through the service of neighbor. She engaged in the care of the poor and the sick and, as her prophetic gifts became known, became a peacemaker between warring cities in Italy. She was influential in freeing the popes who were in Avignon under control of the French king, and through Raymund of Capua she instituted the reform of the Dominican Order by the foundation of houses of strict observance in each province. In our time Pope Paul VI declared her a Doctor of the Church. For spiritual directors the section of Catherine's *Dialogue* in which God the Father answers her questions about how she is to deal with those who come to her for spiritual help is classic, and will be discussed later in this book.

The 1400's saw the so-called Renaissance or rebirth of classical learning. Actually the revival of classical learning had already begun in the High Middle Ages, but then the emphasis had been on science and philosophy, while the Renaissance turned its attention to Latin and Greek literature and art. While the earlier period had been marked by the other-worldly interests of the clergy, this period saw the rise of the laity with more earthly concerns. Contrary to the impression given by some historians, however, the Renaissance remained an intensely Christian age, and the pagan influences were quickly assimilated by the Christian worldview. The need to make this assimilation, however, did raise important questions for Dominican preaching and stimulated a revival of the study of Aquinas, whose *Summa Theologiae* now became the basis of Dominican instruction, under the leadership of John Capreolus (d. 1440), the first of the major Dominican commentators.

Dominican theologians also played important roles at the Council of Constance which ended the scandal of the three popes and dealt with the schism of John Hus, and at the Council of Basle, and also the Council of Ferrara-Florence which almost succeeded in ending the ancient schism of the Eastern Church. Because these councils failed, Islam was able to end the Christian Byzantine Empire.

At the beginning of the century, the great apocalyptic preacher St. Vincent Ferrer (d. 1419) called for reform of the church and played a major role at the Council of Constance. Among his important other works was the *Treatise on the Spiritual Life*, which proposed a very severe asceticism of poverty, silence, and purification of the heart. The policy of Raymond of Capua as Master of the Order to found houses of strict observance was promoted in Italy by Bl. John Dominici (d. 1419), who wrote a famous work, *The Glow Worm*, warning of the risks of basing education on the pagan classics rather than the Bible, and another treatise *On Family Care*. His influence was especially felt in Florence, then the leading city of Italy, and was taken up by St. Antoninus Pierozzi (d. 1459) of Florence, who became its archbishop. His *Summa Moralis*, the first independent treatise of moral theology, dealt with the ethical problems of all classes of the laity, businessmen, physicians, statesmen, etc. Antoninus, noted for his charity to the poor, also wrote a spiritual work, *On Living Well*, and important manuals for confessors which emphasized their role as "physicians of souls."

This reform, however, caused quarrels between the observants and the conventuals, and eventually led the pope to require Dominicans to abandon mendicancy in 1475 and own some revenued property.

Nevertheless, the great Girolamo Savonarola at San Marco in Florence continued the Catherinian spirit of reform not only of his order, but of the church, by his prophetic, even apocalyptic, warnings to the corrupt popes of the period, and especially by a major effort to transform his city into a truly Christian republic where peace and justice might reign. His enemies finally had him burned at the stake (1498). Among his many sermons and other works are treatises on the nature of prophecy, *Compendium of Revelations*, and *Dialogue on Prophetic Truth* with seven visitors from the East whose names spell *Veritas*! He also wrote a very important spiritual work, *On the Simplicity of the Christian Life*, and commentaries on the *Miserere* (written in prison) and on the Our Father, which deals with reading, meditating, praying, and contemplating as phases of prayer.[12] His *Triumph of the Cross* is a powerful work of apologetics.

This prophetic spirit was also exemplified by a number of Dominican women, who followed in the footsteps of St. Catherine, typical of whom was Osanna de Andreasi (d. 1505) who was the spiritual guide of many people in Mantua, including its ruling duchess, Isabella D'Este, and who left an important series of letters of direction to a young priest, Jerome, a Benedictine of the Olivetan Reform. Bl. Lucia of Narnia (d.1544) was the advisor of Ercole I, Duke of Ferrara (Isabella's father) and received miraculous visits from another prophetess, Bl. Catherine of Racconigi (1547), while Bl. Columba of Rieti (d.1501) appeared to Osanna to prepare her for death.

Columba was so famous as a prophetess that the citizens of Narni (who later fought a battle to retain Lucia of Narni in their town) attempted to abduct her to their city, but she escaped to Foligno and then Perugia. She even visited the corrupt pope, Alexander VI, and called him to repentance. Bl. Stephana de Quinzani (d. 1530) of Brescia, a stigmatic, was consulted by Osanna and by the Franciscan tertiary, St. Angela Merici, who was to found the Ursulines, one of the first teaching orders for girls. Domenica del Paradiso (d. 1553) was also a stigmatic, who had visions of Columba. She founded a house of tertiaries with the Dominican habit to which she added the cross of Savonarola, but the Master of the Order, Thomas del Vio, later Cardinal Cajetan, who opposed the enthusiasm for the memory of the prophet, did not recognize her community, and she was able to be professed as a Dominican only when dying at age 79. A similar case in Spain was the remarkable Maria de Santo Domingo, known as the "Beata de Piedrahita" [(d. 1525; (a "beata" was a pious woman, not necessarily a nun)] which occasioned much controversy and an eventual formal investigation in which she was cleared of pious fraud.

This rather odd network of women charismatics played an important role in the Catholic Reformation, to which Savonarola had given so strong an impetus. Thus, St. Catherine de Ricci (d. 1589) a mystic and stigmatic, a friend of St. Philip Neri, left us letters of direction, like those of Catherine of Siena, which exemplify a Savonarolian spirituality. Also the priest Giovanni Battista Carioni da Crema (d. 1534) wrote a work, *On the Love of God and the Holy Hatred of Self*, influenced especially by Cavalca and St. Catherine of Siena. He was a friend of the religious reformers St. Cajetan of Thiene and St. Anthony Zaccaria, who founded the first congregations of clerk regulars, then a new type of religious order in the church.

In northern Europe, more gradually touched by the Renaissance, this period saw much popular writing on spirituality for the laity, such as John Nider's (1438) *On How to Live Well* and *Twenty-Four Golden Harps Showing the Nearest Way to Heaven*, and for the reform of religious life, such as John van Uyt den Hove's *Treatise on the Reform of Religious*. Underlying this growth in Germanic culture, however, was a deep anxiety produced by rapid social change, and it found its expression in the mob hysteria of the great witchcraft craze which swept northern Europe. Theologians attempted to understand this phenomenon and control it, as in the notorious *Malleus Maleficarum (Hammer of Witches*, 1486) of the Dominican inquisitors Heinrich Institoris and Jacob Sprenger (1486), whose theory that witches had made a covenant with the devil probably made matters worse and led to the death of many, mainly women victims. Yet, as Sigmund Freud was later to acknowledge, this demonology initiated the modern interest in the darkside of the human psyche, which today has to be taken into account in any attempt to understand spiritual pathology.

The Rosary and Popular Devotions

The fifteenth century was also a period when the effort to develop a spirituality for the laity led Dominican preachers to center more and more on special devotional practices, of which by far the most important was the rosary of the Blessed Virgin Mary. Its most ardent promoter was Alan de Rupe (de la Roche, d. 1475), who in the 1470's preached the legend that the rosary had been given to Dominic by the Virgin herself, a legend whose foundations are very obscure, since the use of beads in prayer was much older than Dominic. What is certain, however, is that devotion to Mary and prayer to her accompanied by such gestures as genuflections goes back to Dominic and the early days of the order, as noted in the above quotation from *The Lives of the Brethren.* [13]

The rosary henceforth was to become a powerful way of supplying for the laity an equivalent of the hours for the clergy. The first Confraternity of the Rosary was founded at Douai in 1470, and the second by Jacob Sprenger (the same just noted for his pursuit of witches!) at Cologne in 1475. A long line of famous rosary preachers grew up in the order, e.g., Francois Michel (d. 1502) who wrote on the Seven Sorrows of Mary; the Polish Justin de Miechow (d. 1649) who wrote an important treatise on mariology based on the principle of the divine maternity, and Bl. Francisco de Posadas (d. 1713) who sought to expose false mysticism. Devotion to the Holy Name of Jesus also spread among the Dominicans, and St. Pius V entrusted the Holy Name Society to them.

Another emphasis in popular preaching was on the lives and miracles of the saints, which Dominicans had promoted since the famous *Golden Legend* of James of Voragine in the thirteenth century, and which was a source much used by artists in their depiction of the saints. This work eventually helped Ignatius Loyola to conversion and was read by Teresa of Avila.

Many Dominican names occur in the history of Renaissance humanism. At its dawn, Dante, himself a Franciscan tertiary, had listened to the lectures of Remigio de' Girolami, O.P. (d. 1319), a disciple of St. Thomas Aquinas, and had celebrated the memory of Mechtilde of Magdeburg, who as "the Blessed Matilda" meets him in the Earthly Paradise. [14] Bl. James Griesinger of Ulm (d. 1491) was famous as an artist in stained glass. Under the influence of St. Antoninus of Florence, Bl. Fra Angelico (John of Fiesole) painted the luminous frescos in the Dominican novitiate of San Marco, that showed how the arts can also be a means of preaching. A disciple of Savonarola, the Dominican painter Fra Bartolomeo de la Porta (d. 1517) was a friend of Raphael and the other major artists of the time. Plautilla Nelli (d. 1587) was a woman painter of note. Matthew Bandello (d. 1560) was a short-story writer, whose plots Shakespeare was to borrow, and some of the convents of Dominican nuns were known for the plays they wrote and performed. Francisco Colonna authored a famous and fantastic dream novel about architecture, *The Dream of Poliphilio*, and Santes Pagnino (d. 1541) and Sixtus of Siena (d. 1566) were important initiators of philological biblical studies. Tomás de Santa María was a noted music theorist (d. 1570).

Yet at this same time in northern Europe, the inward-looking, subjective spirituality of Germany and the Rhineland, in which Meister Eckhart's mysticism played so big a part, along with the demands for church reform which Catherine and Savonarola had fostered, had developed into the religious individualism of the Protestant schism. The Dominican provinces of Germany and a great number of its nuns were swept away in this one-sided reform. Luther himself, an Augustinian friar, was deeply influenced by Eckhart through the *Conferences* of Tauler and the anonymous *Theologia Germanica* (c. 1350, later edited by Martin Luther) of the same school of mysticism, although he claimed for his thought a purely biblical foundation and rejected Eckhart's Neoplatonic philosophical background. On the other hand, it was a Dominican, John Tetzel, whose popular preaching of indulgences was the occasion of the schism. Yet many other Dominican preachers labored strenuously to overcome the schism and some, like St. John of Gorkum, suffered martyrdom as a result.

The Controversy on Grace

Since the Reformation had its roots in a controversy over the role of grace in Christian life, it concerned a debate over spirituality. At the Council of Trent (1545–1563), which checked the spread of Protestantism, Dominican bishops were highly influential, and the theology of St. Thomas Aquinas on grace was closely followed. Dominicans wrote the *Roman Catechism* which systematized the teachings of the council for the use of preachers. The practical implementation of the council and liturgical reform was initiated by the courageous but severe Dominican pope, St. Pius V (d. 1572). The theology of grace also was the principal topic of debate between the Dominican Thomists, the Franciscan Scotists, and the Suarezians of the newly founded Society of Jesus in what is called baroque or second scholasticism.

Thomas de Vio, Cardinal Cajetan (d. 1534), who had personally debated with Luther, was the leader of the revived Thomism, which was then taken up by Conrad Köllin (d. 1536) in Germany, and especially by a brilliant group in Spain, Francisco Vitoria (d. 1546), Domingo de Soto (d. 1560), Domingo Báñez (leader in the debates over grace, d. 1604) and Melchior Cano (d.1560). St. Teresa of Avila, a Carmelite, found such Dominican spiritual directors as Domingo Báñez, Vicente Barron, Pedro Ibanez, Garcia de Toledo whom she consulted, to be men of great spiritual insight and learning.

Of special significance for spiritual direction (besides the fundamental question of grace) was the controversy over mystical prayer. Archbishop Bartolomé Carranza (d. 1576), primate of Spain and writer of an important catechism for the laity, spent years under investigation by the Inquisition because he was accused of leaning to the subjectivism of the Lutherans. Carranza's chief accuser, Melchior Cano, who wrote a valuable spiritual guide for the laity, was highly suspicious of false mysticism.

One of the first of such "guides" was published by Pierre Doré in Paris in 1546. Most popular of all such works was *The Sinner's Guide* of Luis of Granada (d. 1588), a noted spiritual director (although sadly deceived by one notorious nun who falsely claimed the stigmata). In this much-copied *Guide*, he steered a sane middle course in the controversy over infused prayer and was probably the most prolific and influential spiritual writer of the century, but there were many other Spanish Dominicans writing in this field, such as Bartholomew of the Martyrs (d. 1590), author of a notable and often translated *Compendium of Spiritual Teaching*, and Jean de Lazcano, whose *On prayer and meditation* (Pamplona, 1630) discussed, along with meditation for the interior good of soul, fasting for the good of the body, and almsgiving with regard to exterior goods.

The Moral Systems Controversy

The Catholic Reformation and the baroque church dominated Italy, France and Spain in the seventeenth century, definitively separated from the Protestantism of northern Europe by terrible religious wars and the principle of *cuius regio, cuius religio*, the union of church and state under absolute monarchies. Internally the Dominican Order took on this same pattern in which much of its democratic character was obscured by centralization of power in the Master of the Order and his curia, with infrequent general chapters. The immense success of the Society of Jesus in this period caused its spirituality to influence all the other religious orders deeply. This was true also of the Order of Preachers in which the reform of Raymund of Capua had largely completed its work with the triumph of the observants over the conventuals, as in the sometimes stormy reforms in France of Sebastien Michaelis (d. 1618) and Antoine Le Quieu (d. 1676).

This was also the time of the rise of modern science with the work of Galileo in physics, Harvey in biology, and of the "turn to the subject" in the philosophy of Descartes. Cartesian rationalism began gradually to supplant baroque scholasticism. A few Dominicans, such as Giordano Bruno (d. 1600) who ended as a pantheist and was burned at the stake, and Thomas Campanella (d. 1639), a supporter of Galileo and a political reformer who wrote the famous utopian, *The City of the Sun*, struck out on new paths. Most Dominicans, however, seemed not fully aware of such new trends. Their energies were still absorbed in the last phases of the controversy over grace and free will, but most of all in a new controversy with the Jesuits on the question of *moral systems*.

This debate, which also has a direct relation to spirituality, resulted from the fact that the Jesuits, following their chief theologian, Suarez, had adopted the Franciscan Scotistic view of *voluntarism* in moral theology, according to which it is the will of the legislator, whether God or man, that determines what is right or wrong, in contrast to the Thomistic view that right and wrong are determined by the objective relation of means to ends in human life as perceived in God's wisdom, in which we participate by revelation and by reason. In other words, something is morally bad not because God wills it to be so, but it is against his will because it is in fact harmful for his beloved creatures.

Today most moral theologians seem to be returning to the Thomistic conception in reaction to the legalism that tended to dominate Catholic morality in the period after Trent, but in this period the voluntaristic view seemed more understandable to people used to living under a centralized government in church and state. The Jesuits, seeking to mediate between defending the authority of church teaching against

Protestantism and the pastoral need to encourage frequent confession, taught that one might in practice follow the easier opinion in a moral controversy if some reliable Catholic theologians defended it as at least *probable*. Dominicans, on the contrary, generally thought it unreasonable to follow any but the *more probable* view as to the effective means to an end. This controversy continued into the eighteenth century, particularly in the works of Daniel Concina, O.P. (d. 1756) which received much papal support.

The reform movement in France called *Jansenism* (after a Dutch theologian who had sought to revive the teachings of Augustine on grace), often represented itself as Thomist in its opposition to Jesuit casuistry. In 1653 Pope Innocent X condemned Jansenism; in 1687 Innocent XII condemned the false mysticism of Molinos, and in 1699 Innocent XIII condemned the quietism of Fénelon. Dominicans, like the Jesuits, opposed the moral rigorism of Jansenism, with its pessimistic view of human nature, although Jansenists sometimes claimed Thomistic support on the question of predestination; and both Jesuits and Dominicans wrote against quietism. Among its Dominican opponents were Thomas Du Jardin (d. 1733), who made much use of the works of Tauler, and the Thomistic commentator Charles-René Billuart (d. 1757).

Dominican Thomists acknowledged the legitimate claims of humanism, as is evident from the many Dominican works of literature written in this period, by their preaching of the rosary with its meditation on the humanity of Jesus and Mary, and by their engagement in the arts, for example the painting of the Spaniard, Juan Mayno (d. 1646) and the South American Pedro Bedon (d. 1621).

The Call to Mysticism Controversy

Important theologians of the seventeenth century were Thomas Lemos (d. 1629) prominent in the grace controversy; Jean Poinsot (John of St. Thomas, d. 1644) a major commentator on St. Thomas and initiator of the branch of philosophy called semiotics, who wrote a very important spiritual treatise, *On the Seven Gifts of the Holy Spirit*; John Baptist Gonet (d. 1681); another Thomistic commentator, Giacinto Passerini (d. 1677) noted for his work *On the States of Life* (although some of his works were put on the Index for quietist tendencies); and

Vincent Contenson (d. 1674), author of a *Theology of Mind and Heart* which deals extensively with spirituality.

The title of Contenson's work is indicative of a trend in what is often called the French School of Spirituality, toward a greater concern for the subjective experiences met in prayer, and a resurgence of the Eckhartian tradition emphasizing detachment and passivity to the action of grace. In some writers this led to the quietism against which Tauler had warned much earlier. The Dominican writers of the seventeenth century struggled to find a balance between Jansenistic moralism and quietism.

Among the many Dominican spiritual writers of the period were Ignazio Del Nente (d. 1648), strongly influenced by Henry Suso, who wrote *On the Peace of the Soul in the Light of Nature, Faith, Wisdom and Divine Love*, and promoted devotion to the Sacred Heart of Jesus; Thomas de Vallgornera (d. 1662) who wrote a notable, but not very original, *Mystical Theology of St. Thomas Aquinas*; Archbishop Nicolas Coeffeteau (d. 1623) who wrote against Calvinism and on human emotions and the capital sins; Louis Chardon (d. 1651) whose famous work on *The Cross of Jesus* studied the inner life of Jesus in the perspective of his recognition of his ultimate sacrificial death; and Alexander Piny (d. 1709) who in his *The Prayer of the Heart* opposed quietism, but defended the universal call to contemplation. Some French Dominicans, however, were much more cautious. Antonin Massoulié (d. 1706) who wrote a *Treatise on True Prayer*, a *Treatise on the Love of God*, and completed Contenson's *Meditations of St. Thomas Aquinas* on the three ways of the spiritual life, and Jean Francois Billecocq (d. 1711) in his *Familiar Instructions on True Devotion: The Perfect Christian in the World*, were reluctant to open the way to quietism or "enthusiasm" and so urged the laity to follow the "ordinary way" of perfection.

The influence of Dominican women also increased during this period. Hippolyte de Jesus (d. 1624), niece of a Master of the Order, Juan Tomás de Rocaberti, published no less than twenty-two folio volumes of spiritual writings, which, however, were put on the *Index of Forbidden Books*, "until corrected." Juliana Morrell (d. 1653), a prodigy of learning as a young girl, who became a nun, translated into French and commented the *Treatise on the Spiritual Life* of St. Vincent Ferrer, and wrote other spiritual works. Ven. Agnes de Jesus (d. 1634), a stigmatic, constantly aware of the presence of her guardian angel, was important in the development of the French School of spirituality. She was a friend of Jean-Jacques Olier, founder of the Sulpicians, and encouraged him in the development of the seminary system for educating priests.

Most notable of all at this time was St. Louis Grignion de Montfort, who founded his own congregations of priests and sisters, but also belonged to the Dominican family and was a great preacher of the rosary. His chief works, aimed at Jansenistic rationalism, were *True Devotion to the Blessed Virgin Mary* and his *The Love of Eternal Wisdom*, modeled after a similar work by Bl. Henry Suso, in which St. Louis proposed four means to attain wisdom: (1) to desire it; (2) to pray for it constantly; (3) to prepare for it by detachment from all created goods; (4) to consecrate oneself to the Blessed Virgin Mary, Mother of Wisdom. A Neapolitan Dominican, Seraphin Brienza (d. 1752) wrote a work on St. Thomas as spiritual director, *The Renunciation of Self*, influenced by Tauler and Suso, which carefully distinguished between the true and false self.

Underlying all the controversies of this century was a central issue: Are there two different ways of the Christian life: the ordinary way of most Christians, consisting in obedience to the commandments, vocal prayer, and active meditation; and an extraordinary way of mystical contemplative prayer? From this distinction arose an accepted dichotomy in seminaries between *ascetic* and *mystical* theology.

Throughout the eighteenth and nineteenth centuries the theory of the ordinary and extraordinary ways of grace gained general acceptance, and was especially favored by Jesuit authors. It was popularized by Jean-Baptiste Scaramelli, S.J. (d. 1752), but seems to have first been proposed in 1676 by the Polish Franciscan, Chrysostom Dobrosielski. This question, which I will discuss later, has again been raised in the twentieth century.

The Rights of Humanity

After the Spanish entered the Americas, the theologians Francisco Vitoria and Domingo de Soto, and the great missionaries Antonio Montesinos (d. 1530) and Bartolomé de las Casas (d. 1566), basing their arguments on Aquinas' doctrine of natural law, became the defenders of international law, human rights, and especially the rights of the Native Americans. Their views have been fundamental to the contemporary church's teaching on social justice and to modern liberation theology.

In the missions in the New World and the Far East, this was a period of great expansion, and produced numerous Dominican martyrs. In China, the Dominicans and Franciscans, however, opposed the Jesuit policy of enculturation which they saw, mistakenly it would now seem, as compromising the gospel (the Rites Controversy). Of special interest are the stories of Saints Rose of Lima, Martin de Porres (African-Indian in origin) and John Massias in Lima, Peru who engaged in social work, carrying on the ideals of Las Casas.

Secularism

What had seemed the triumph of the Catholic Reformation soon turned sour in the eighteenth century. The religious wars had raised serious religious doubts in the minds of intellectuals, and after 1650 a growing spirit of skepticism and fideism was apparent in Europe among the elite. The Enlightenment, therefore, rejected the Christian revelation and sought to build a new culture based on pure reason and the technological control of the world through the new science. This first developed in England where religion was at a low ebb as the result of the wars between the Puritans and the Established church, while the new science was at a high tide as the result of the work of Isaac Newton (an Arian in religion). This rationalistic and deistic worldview passed to the American colonies, where it colored the thought of our Founding Fathers, and to France in more radical and even atheistic form where it eventually resulted in the French Revolution and the tyrannical empire of Napoleon Bonaparte.

These events were devastating to the church and to the Dominican Order, which had been too absorbed in the controversies over grace, probabilism, and Jansenism to be intellectually prepared to meet it. Throughout Europe, and especially in France, vocations to the religious life declined drastically during the eighteenth century. The number of Dominican friars fell from 30,000, its historic high point, at the beginning of the century, to less than 4000 at its end.

Under these circumstances the order tended to be backward-looking, indulging itself nostalgically in historical studies. This was a time of a growing interest in church history, partly as a result of controversies with the Protestants over the nature of the early church. Jacques Goar (d. 1653) and Michel le Quien (d. 1676) studied the liturgy and history of the Eastern churches, and Nicholas Coffeteau (d. 1623) was a noted linguist. Jacques Quetif and Jacques Echard in 1724 finished a monumental biographical and bibliographical work on *The Writers of the Order of Preachers* down to 1700. Thomas Soueges wrote the *Année Dominicaine* on the lives of the saints of the order, and Antoine Touron its history, while Thomas Mamachi and Noel Alexander (d. 1724), and Joseph Augustine Orsi wrote church histories. But almost the only important work in philosophy was Salvatore Roselli's anti-Cartesian textbook on philosophy. Charles Louis Richard (d. 1794—killed in the revolution) countered the *Encyclopédie* of Voltaire, which was the Bible of the Enlightenment, with his *Universal Dictionary of the Sacred Sciences.*

There were some noted thinkers also, such as Charles René Billuart (d. 1757), a Thomistic commentator, Joseph Galien (d. 1783) a scientist and inventor, and especially Daniel Concina (d. 1756) whose opposition to probabilism led to extensive works on moral theology and the history of ascetic discipline in the church.

It was a period of extensive missionary work and of many martyrs in the Far East. Although the Dominican women of this time also suffered from the Enlightenment persecution, they produced Mary Rose Giannini (d. 1741) a laywoman and notable mystic, Deodata del Divino Amore (d. 1754) a spiritual writer, and Cecilia Mayer (1749) who offered her whole life of prayer for the survival of the church in those difficult years. Most significant for the future was Bl. Mother Marie Poussepin, who founded the Sisters of Charity of the Presentation, one of the first of the active sisterhoods which were to flourish in the next century. Others, such as the laywoman Catherine Jarrige (d. 1836) worked in the underground during the French Revolution saving the lives of priests and other Catholics from the Terror.

Revival of the Order and of Thomism

The 1800's saw the church at its most embattled. After the decline of Napoleon's empire it faced militantly secularist governments. The church, however, began to regain its balance with Vatican Council I

(1870) under Pius IX, which defined papal authority and the relation of faith and reason, and with the encyclical *Aeterni Patris* (1879) of Leo XIII, which made the philosophy and theology of St. Thomas Aquinas the basis of Catholic education.

At the beginning of this period the order was almost dead in Europe, with the Spanish section of the order practically separated from the rest of the order from 1804–1876. However, a native of Maryland, Dominic Fenwick (d. 1832) established the first foundation in the United States in 1805, from which came the Spaniard Joseph Sadoc Alemany (d. 1888), first archbishop in California and founder of another United States province, and the great missionary Ven. Samuel Mazzuchelli (1849). So devastated was the order in Europe that a zealous preacher like Bl. Francisco Coll (d. 1875), who had made his profession in 1830, was forced to live almost his whole religious life as a preacher without a community after the government had closed all religious houses in 1835. Henri Lacordaire (d. 1861), another great preacher, refounded the order in France in 1850. He explained his reasons to the French public in an eloquent *Memoir* in which he wrote:[15]

> You may perhaps ask why we have chosen to re-establish an old order rather than to found a new one. We shall give two answers. First, the grace to be the founder of an order is the highest and most exceptional that God gives to his saints, and it has not been given to us. And secondly, if God were to grant us the power to create a new religious order, we are aware that, after much reflection, we should discover nothing newer or more adapted to our time and its needs than the rule of St. Dominic.

Notable among Lacordaire's writings are his *Letters to Young Men* which show him as a spiritual guide very sensitive to the needs of his time. Under the leadership of Vincent Jandel (d. 1872), a companion of Lacordaire but more monastic-minded, the Order of Preachers had expanded again to thirty provinces. The monastic emphasis of Jandel continued into the twentieth century in such writers as the saintly Hyacinthe Cormier (d. 1916), a Master of the Order, expressed in his *Instruction of Novices*.

By the end of the century, the order was once more producing great scholars, such as Tommaso Zigliara (d. 1893) a leader in the Thomistic renewal, Henrich Denifle (d. 1905) the medievalist responsible for renewed interest in the Rhineland mystics, Zephyrinus Gonzalez (d. 1894) a historian of philosophy, Jacques Marie Monsobré, a great preacher, Hyacinth Besson (d. 1861) a noted artist, and Bertrand Wilberforce (d. 1904) an English spiritual writer.

New Roles for Women

Even more remarkable than the revival of the men's order, however, was the astonishing growth of the Dominican active sisterhoods ("Third Order Religious"). Up to this time women in the order (with a few exceptions) had been Second Order nuns, or Third Order lay-women living at home, like St. Catherine, or gathered in communities like that of St. Catherine de Ricci, which led a cloistered life hardly distinguishable from that of the nuns. Now these Third Order communities, while seeking to retain much of the pattern of cloistered life, launched out into active ministries in education, hospitals, and social work. For Dominican sisters, teaching in Christian schools tended to be the predominant work.

These active sisterhoods spread throughout Europe and the missions. In the United States the sisters were founded in Kentucky by Dominic Fenwick and Mother Angela Sansbury (d. 1839). Samuel Mazzuchelli and Mother Emily Powers (d. 1909) founded the sisters of Sinsinawa, Wisconsin. Many United States congregations originated in the thirteenth-century monastery of Ratisbon (Regensburg) associated with St. Albert the Great. These included the foundation by Mother Benedict Bauer (d. 1865), in Brooklyn and then Amityville, in 1853, and Racine, in 1862, spreading from Amityville to Newburg, 1869, Grand Rapids, 1877, Caldwell, 1881, San José, 1888, Great Bend, 1902; from Newburg, Blauvelt, 1890, Tacoma, 1892, Adrian, 1923, Edmonds 1923; and from Caldwell, Akron, 1929.

In England Mother Margaret Hallahan (d. 1868) was the foundress, and Mother Frances Raphael Drane (d. 1893) was a novelist and historian of the order. In all, some thirty-four congregations of sisters were founded in this century and played a major role in the expansion of the church worldwide. The tensions inherent in their attempt to retain the pattern of cloistered life while engaging in the active apostolate, however, were never resolved during this time.

Before and After Vatican II

In this century, Dominican life has been divided into two halves by the Second Vatican Council (1963–1965). The first of these was marked by the continued expansion of the active sisterhoods, especially into mission lands, such as the communities founded by Dr. Agnes McLaren (d. 1913) of the Medical Missionaries, Mother Mary Joseph Rogers (d. 1955) of the Maryknoll Sisters; Mother Alphonsa Hawthorne (daughter of the famous novelist, d. 1926) of the Sisters for the Care of the Cancerous Poor, etc. During this same time the men's order grew notably, both in its missionary activities and its devotion to the Thomistic revival. At the beginning of that revival an eclectic neo-scholasticism was mistaken for authentic Thomism. Soon, also, attempts such as that of the Transcendental Thomists to blend Thomism and modern Kantian philosophy became popular, under the leadership of Joseph Maréchal, S.J. The Dominicans, such as Norbert del Prado (d. 1918), Edouard Hugon (d. 1929), and Reginald Garrigou-Lagrange (d. 1964), however, were concerned with Thomas' own thought, its metaphysical basis, and its major Dominican commentators. Others sought to place it in historical context and to apply it to current problems, such as Pierre Mandonnet (1946), M. H. Vicaire (d. 1993), M.D. Chenu (b. 1895), Yves Congar (b. 1904), Francisco Marin-Sola (d. 1932) Santiago Ramirez (d. 1967) along with whom should be mentioned two laymen closely associated with Dominicans, Jacques Maritain (d. 1973), and Étienne Gilson. One of the most significant achievements of the century was the foundation of the École Biblique in Jerusalem by the great exegete M. J. Lagrange (d. 1938), the leader in reconciling the historical-critical method with the church's doctrine on biblical inspiration.

Another movement, especially pertinent to this book, was the revival of the old controversy, mentioned earlier, about whether there are two ways of the Christian spiritual life, one ordinary and one extraordinary. Prominent among the critics of the two-way theory were the Dominicans Juan Arintero (d. 1928, now a candidate for beatification), a Spaniard, and Reginald Garrigou-Lagrange, a Frenchman who in magisterial works on the spiritual life argued that all Christians are called to attain contemplative prayer, since this is only the flowering of the gifts of the Holy Spirit given to all in baptism.

This encouragement of the laity to seek the heights of contemplation was fostered by the publication of journals devoted to the spiritual life. Arintero founded *La Vida Sobrenatural*, the French *La Vie Spirituelle*, the Italians the *Rivisita di Ascetica e Mistica*, the Americans *Cross and Crown* (later *Spirituality Today*). The theological basis of these journals was supplied by the work of Arintero and Garrigou-Lagrange, but also by the writings of Ambroise Gardeil (d. 1931) who studied the psychology of faith. Dominicans who presented the Dominican tradition in a more popular vein included, in Germany, Albert M. Weiss (d. 1925); Hieronymus Wilms (d. 1978); and G.G. Meersemann (b. 1903); in France Antonin Sertillanges (d. 1948), author of over four hundred works; in England Bede Jarrett (d. 1934), Vincent McNabb (d. 1943), the street-preacher; Gerald Vann (d. 1963), known especially for his *The Heart of Man* and *The Divine Pity*; in the lowlands, Valentine Walgrave, and Edward Schillebeeckx; and in the United States, Walter Farrell (d. 1951), Jordan Aumann and Paul Hinnebusch.

This intense scholarly work undoubtedly played a major role in the preparation of Vatican II, and many of the themes of the council had previously been developed by Dominicans, such as Lagrange's ideas in biblical studies, Congar's on ecumenism and the role of the laity in the church, Schillebeeckx's on the church as a sacrament, Garrigou-Lagrange on the universal call to holiness. Nevertheless, the council also opened the way to theological pluralism and put an end to the hegemony of Thomistic theology, although continuing to approve it as a safe guide. Although Dominican historical studies have done much to promote a more historical approach in theology, the Thomistic emphasis on the objectivity of truth now has to compete with modern philosophies stressing subjective factors in knowledge.

Moreover, the French provinces which had led the intellectual life in the first half of the century, but had become involved in the priest-worker movement, now were deeply affected by the concern for social justice and by Marxist thought which characterized the student movement of 1968 and which later took the form of liberation theology. It seems that what the church now needed was to become more deeply involved in the social problems of the world. Yet the preservation and exposition of the church's full doctrinal heritage remains a Dominican concern, and a Dominican, Christoph von Schönborn was chosen by

Pope John Paul II to execute the difficult task of supervising the preparation of the *Catechism of the Catholic Church* (1992).

Yet, although Vatican II was a sign of hope in our troubled times, the changes it sought to bring about were often misunderstood. A marked decline of priestly and religious life in the more secularized countries, has deeply affected the Dominican Order. Among the sisters in the United States this has been precipitous. Many congregations, especially in the United States, have put off the religious habit, turned from schools and hospitals to social work, with a dispersion of younger membership to small communities, or even the abandonment of community life. A major issue for Dominican sisters has become what assimilation to make of the feminist views emanating from the contemporary women's movement. Among the men, many also left the Order to marry, especially in late 1960's and early 1970's, and many live outside a community in order to carry on a great variety of ministries more as an individual rather than common tasks.

This crisis resembles in many respects that of the eighteenth century and is undoubtedly a phase in the church's struggle with an increasingly secularist society. But at the same time the order is involved in extensive missionary work in over eighty countries and is moving into an epoch of global pluralism and ecumenism. The Enlightenment worldview which for two hundred years has dominated the developed countries is now challenged by "post-modernism" and the opportunities for the ministry of the word for which the order was founded are immense. The survival of the order, which is only an instrument of the church, depends on whether this crisis leads to a deepening of its spirituality and its commitment to the ministry of the word in the service of the church, as St. Dominic intended.

Chapter 2

Created in the Divine Image

The Human Person

The first question those who assume the responsibility of directing the spiritual life of others must ask themselves is: *"Who is this person who is asking my guidance on her or his way to God?"* Every person is unique and must be understood in his or her own terms, yet this is not possible unless we view this individual in the context of what all human beings have in common. The classic analysis of this common human nature to be found in the Dominican tradition (but not the only one) is that given by St. Thomas Aquinas. In the following two chapters I will try to give a brief account of this anthropology, comparing it sometimes to those of other thinkers in the same tradition, with emphasis on the relevance of this analysis to spiritual growth. Aquinas carefully distinguishes human nature as such, from its deformation by sin and its transformation by grace. In this chapter I will deal only with nature, and in the next chapter with its transformations by sin and by grace.

As a philosopher Aquinas studied human nature empirically by observing human behavior, and distinguished in it five dimensions: the physical, the biological, the psychological, the ethical, and the spiritual. I use the term "dimension" because, just as in a mathematical space any point can be located only in reference to three or more dimensional coordinates, so to describe any event in human behavior we have to refer to all five of these dimensions of the human person.

The Physical Dimension of the Human Person

When we meet somebody new and are trying to identify them, one of the first questions we ask is, "Where do you live? Where are you from?" The very first chapters of the Bible locate Adam and Eve in the

33

Garden of Eden on the earth and under the heavens, before they relate the spiritual journey of our race. To understand the persons we are directing on their spiritual journey we must also begin by locating them in the universe, in their ecology, their home—or homelessness—and ask ourselves the question: *Where does this person live in God's creation?*

Christian spirituality has been deeply influenced in its understanding of the human person by two Greek philosophers, Plato and Aristotle. Aquinas decisively opted for Aristotle's view of the human person, while striving to assimilate to this Aristotelian model whatever was of value Plato had taught him. For Plato the human person is really the soul, the intelligence and will. The body is merely a temporary garment the soul puts on as it descends from the heavens to earth, and which it will abandon as it reascends to the spiritual realm. It is the cause of the soul's forgetfulness of its true home and a burden and a hindrance to its return to its celestial home. Although the body is a beautiful manifestation of the soul and hence a reminder of the superior beauty of the soul, it only recalls us to seek to escape imprisonment in matter.

St. Thomas rejected this conception as incompatible with the Christian doctrines of the resurrection, and preferred Aristotle's non-dualistic view that soul and body are complementary as matter and form. The matter of a pot is a mere lump of clay until it is formed, but the form of a pot not embodied in clay cannot hold water. Thomas, of course, held that the body exists for the sake of the soul, but without it, the soul, although it continues to exist after death, is no longer a *person*, able to learn and to perform free acts.

Hence, for Aquinas the human person is in our experience, first of all, a part of the material world of stars and planets and earth subject to its natural laws in a process of constant change. Although Thomas' scientific views of the structure of the physical world were far more primitive than ours, they were derived from reasoning based on empirical facts, not on myths or mere speculation. They led him to believe that the world is governed by laws accessible to human reason and that the human person cannot exist or be understood apart from its natural environment which constitutes an ecology which we can cultivate and perfect through technology, but only if we respect and conserve its natural balance. Hence, spiritual direction must not be spiritualistic, i.e., it must not try to abstract the person from bodily existence and ecological environment. Where we live and how we treat our bodies are fundamental to right human living and to the proper growth of the person. The director must understand the effect of environment and bodily well-being on every aspect of the client's personal growth. We ought to visit, or at least inquire about the places in which they live and work.

The Biological Dimension of the Human Person

As we become acquainted with someone we often ask, "How do you do? How are you today?" The spiritual director needs to ask the same question, *"How is your health, your bodily condition?"*

Among the bodies that compose the ordered universe as God created it, only some are alive, and among these the most complex of all are human persons. Life is the power of self-movement by which plants nourish themselves, grow and repair injuries, and reproduce their species. The human body has these plant-like or physiological powers by which in a marvelous way it develops from a tiny embryo into the magnificent, adult female or male body. It is subject to the biological rhythms of sleep and waking, of the seasons, of infancy, youth, adulthood, and old age, yet it has remarkable powers of recuperation and healing from injuries and resistance to attacks and disease.

Plants have either the power of asexual reproduction by the division of the organism into two or more individuals, or of sexual reproduction by the combination of genetic materials from two sexually differentiated parents. Sexual reproduction is higher in the evolutionary scale because the combination of genetic material from two different parents results in greater variety among the offspring, and this enables the species to maintain a better ecological balance and promotes evolution so as to adapt life to new or changing environments. Of the two parents the female supplies the egg which contains the material for the further growth of the new organism, while the male parent supplies the sperm which furnishes the extra energy to cause the egg to begin development and also determines that both male and female offspring will be produced. This differentiation of the sexes gives rise to the specifically human institution of the family, and it is essential in understanding human beings and the process of their growth to ask about the family which has been their fundamental environment.

In understanding the behavior of persons we must remember that when these natural powers are weakened or disturbed, the higher and more specific human functions suffer, and we cannot expect the same level of integrated behavior from those who are sick or disabled. For example, a spiritual director must be able to recognize that a client's depression (Aquinas' recognized this condition as *melancholia*) may not be the result of any moral fault, but is simply due to a physiological state which requires time and perhaps medical treatment in order to recover normalcy. It has become more and more evident that the hallucinations of schizophrenics are not "visions" but a physiological disorder that makes it difficult for the patient to distinguish between imagination and reality.

The French Dominican, and experienced director, Fr. A. D. Sertillanges in his well-known book, *The Intellectual Life*, after enthusiastically recommending the pursuit of truth, insists that this requires good health,[16]

> To sum up, you must understand that for an intellectual care of the body, which is the instrument of the soul, is virtue and wisdom; St. Thomas explicitly assigns (*Contra Gentes* III, 141) this character to it, and includes this wisdom for the body amongst the elements that contribute to temporal beatitude, the first beginning of the other beatitude. Do not turn into a wizened and stunted creature, a failure, who later on might be dull-witted, an old man before the time, and therefore, a foolish steward of the talents entrusted to him by the Master. But the care of our bodily partner includes other elements also....If one remains lazy, a glutton, a slave of the pillow and of the table; if one abuses wine, alcohol, tobacco; if one forgets oneself among unwholesome excitements, clinging to habits that are both debilitating and nerve-exhausting, to sins that are perhaps periodically forgiven, but of which the effects remain, how can one practice the hygiene of which we have urged the necessity? A lover of pleasure is an enemy of his body and therefore quickly becomes an enemy of his soul. Mortification of the senses is necessary for thought, and can alone bring us to the *state of clear vision*....If you obey the flesh, you are on the way to become flesh, whereas you must become all spirit.

The Psychological Dimension of the Human Person

The popular psychology of our day has made most spiritual directors aware that in order to understand those they guide it is essential to ask not only the question, *How do you feel about that? but also How do you see, your, world and yourself? What is your fantasy life? What are your significant memories?* since it is our inner world of how we sense, feel, fantasize, remember, picture the future, of sights, sounds, feelings, smells, tastes, images of past and future that begin to reveal the person who lives behind the mask.

For Aquinas animals differ from plants in that they not only have internal processes, but these processes are to some degree guided by their cognitive abilities, the ability to acquire information about their environment and themselves. All animals have at least organs by which they have the sense of touch, and higher animals such as the human person have also organs of taste, smell, hearing, and sight (the external senses).

Moreover, they not only take in data about the external environment, they process this information internally, integrating the information from the different senses, recording it and recalling it when needed, comparing and combining it imaginatively, and responding to it according to inborn instincts or learned patterns (the internal senses: memory and recall, imagination, common sense, and instinct). Although nature furnishes animals with many innate forms of action (instincts), the higher animals are able to incorporate learning experiences as modifications of these broader and more generalized instincts. Thus a dog can learn to perform its instinctual hunting behavior in a learned manner. In animals, as the data of the outer senses is unified by the commonsense, so the data of the internal senses and the total behavior of the animal is unified by its instincts and modified by learning.

But an animal does not have only cognitive abilities, it also has affective abilities, "drives" which move it to seek what it perceives in the light of instinct (innate or modified by learning) as pleasant and to avoid what it perceives as painful. Thus an emotion is a "drive" which results from some image in the internal senses but which causes a physiological change in the animal's body, such as the secretion of hormones, the stiffening or relaxation of muscles, etc., preparing it to react appropriately to some stimulus. This physical change is not directly cognitive, but the change it effects in the body is sensed as an "emotion." For example, an image of danger arouses a drive to escape for which the preparation is a discharge of adrenalin in the blood, a rise in heart beat, a tensing of muscles in preparation to run, and these bodily changes are felt subjectively as the emotion we call "fear."

The great positive theologian of the sixteenth century, Melchior Cano, in his work of spiritual guidance, *Victory Over Self* explained:[17]

> The sensitive part [of human nature], moreover, has two qualities, the irascible and the concupiscent. The latter longs for those sensual delights which are established for the body's sustenance as well as the preservation of the human race. Like a guard and support for its companion, the irascible quality exists to oppose what is harmful, to foster what is healthful. For if the pleasure which exists in sensual things did not awaken concupiscence, then the flesh, which is delicate, weak and hostile to exertion, would cease searching even for what is necessary to support life, since there are so many obstacles to obtaining the essentials. Furthermore, if there were no righteous wrath to protect the good which the individual already possesses, then weak flesh could not long maintain itself among so many hostile forces. Therefore both qualities are necessary. Yet if reason does not guide them with exceptional skill, then, like two runaway horses which are pulling a cart without any brake or rein, they will of necessity destroy themselves and whatever they are carrying along with them. In this case man will not only be like a beast but even worse, since he does not avail himself of that quality which is most important in itself—reason—but instead uses it for his own annihilation.

These drives fall into two groups. The first are the drives to seek pleasure and avoid pain (pleasure-pain drives), which result in the emotions we call: 1) attraction, then (2) desire, and finally, if we move to the pleasurable object and achieve it, (3) enjoyment. Or if, the object is painful, we feel 4) dislike, then (5) withdrawal, and finally, if we cannot escape the pain, (6) grief. But there is a second group of emotions needed by an animal to enable it to attack obstacles that hinder the attainment of pleasure or threaten pain, even if this attack involves risk of some pain (provided it is less than the pleasure sought); these are the aggressive, which result in the emotions of (7) hope to overcome the threatened pain; (8) actual aggression. If the animal is the winner in the struggle, aggression ends in enjoyment, but if it thinks it may lose, then (8) fear is felt; while if it thinks it is losing, then (9) despair. If it has already suffered pain, but has not yet completely yielded to despair, the resultant emotion we call anger. Despair, however, ends in grief. This repertoire of emotions can occur in many subtle combinations, but makes up the emotional life of the animal.

In the waking state of an animal, therefore, there is an inner life of perceptive experiences, some arising from external sensations of the world without and of inner bodily events, and others from internal events in the inner senses and especially from the bodily experiences resulting from the various drives. But higher animals also have periods of sleep and dreaming in which the experiences of the day and of the past are aroused in the inner senses and emotional drives have a certain degree of expression.

When awake the animal reacts to experiences in ways that are appropriate, either from instinct or from learning, but also may react inappropriately in unusual situations, or when suffering from "mental illness," i.e., due to disease of the sense organs, or perhaps to abnormal experiences or training. Its behavior is possible because of its powers of locomotion, moving the body to pursue food, to fight its foes, to seek and copulate with a mate, to care for its young, etc.

The organ of internal sensation which integrates the entire physiology and behavior of an animal is the brain (the ancients, as we can note in the Bible, and medievals like Aquinas thought it was the "heart") along with the central nervous system and the endocrine glands that secrete hormones.

The human person is an animal, but of markedly different behavior than other animals reflected in the human physical structure, especially in that humans have an organ of internal sensations, the brain, which is far more complex than in any other animal. In behavior, human beings are characterized by having only very generalized instincts and must depend mainly on learned behavior; hence, on a culture which they have created and which varies markedly from place to place. Culture also undergoes remarkable changes in time, which generally, but by no means always, are marked by increased human control through technology over the environment and by social organization over human behavior. The most important feature of culture is language (the so-called languages of other animals never result in nature in anything but sounds which express warning, mating, etc.) which makes human beings social animals not by mere instinct but by the voluntary formation of families and more complete societies with an appropriate division and specialization of labor.

The human body is expressive of our difference from other animals. Erect posture enables us to use our senses more flexibly and frees our arms and our flexible hands to manipulate things very delicately. Our bodies are naked to increase our sensitivity to our environment, notably in intimate relationships with other persons, and our culture enables us to protect our nakedness by clothing and shelter.

But it would be a mistake to think that we are able to form cultures and languages merely because we have a bigger brain and thus better internal senses. Invention, language, and sociality, imply that we are not only conscious of the objects of our senses, but that we are self-conscious, that we not only know, but know that we know, and can recognize our selfhood and thus relate to other selves. These kinds of behavior, especially our development of the sciences on which technology depends shows that we are able to think, not merely in images, but in abstract concepts freed of all the particularities of space and time. This means that human knowledge, although dependent for all its data on the bodily senses, is able to transcend the spatial-temporal limitations of matter, and hence is not an organic power, but a non-material power which only uses the brain and senses as instruments, our built-in computer. Therefore, we human persons, although we are the least of spiritual creatures, since we are so utterly dependent on our frail material bodies to learn or do anything, nevertheless are primarily spiritual beings and only secondarily, although essentially and necessarily, material ones.

Yet in understanding the human person we must always begin with an understanding of the human body and its functions. It is through the body that we come to understand the inner human being. The appearance, the body language of a person cannot be neglected in counseling, although it can be superficially deceptive unless we observe it carefully. Moreover, in a Thomistic anthropology, the health of individuals, their physiological balance, their genetic history, are extremely important in understanding their souls. Hence, the spiritual director should try to understand the bodily condition and temperamental peculiarities of the client. Ideally a spiritual director works with a medical doctor, since each contributes to the other an understanding of the person in her or his unique individuality.

For Aquinas, unlike Plato and, in modern philosophy, Descartes and the whole tradition of idealism that stems from him down to the "transcendental Thomists," our self-knowledge does not begin by looking inward at our mental processes, but outward at the material world of which our bodies are a part, and then step by step coming to understand how we are persons. Thus we first consider ourselves as animal, then by contrast with other animals come to see ourselves as distinctly human. Like the animals we also have affective powers, drives or emotions. But the fact that we are intelligent and can therefore think in terms of goals and alternate means, gives us the power of free will by which we can control our behavior, not merely follow instinct or learned patterns of behavior, and this gives rise to the ethical dimension of human nature.

Modern behavioral science has much to say about the way in which our human freedom is limited by the culture in which we have been educated and the patterns of behavior we have learned, as well as by the human unconscious or subconscious mind. By this notion of the unconscious is meant that our memories store up the events and drives and emotions of the past which sometimes rise spontaneously to the threshold of our conscious mind (the ego). Thus they color our perception of the present and influence our behavior without our being clearly aware of them or how to put them into words. Every counselor knows that what troubled clients first declare to be their problems often turn out to be not the real problems at all, but only the cover of some deeper fear that the clients cannot or dare not put into words. Thus, our mental life has many levels descending from what is clearly conscious and expressible to many other deeper things on the border of consciousness.

The teaching of Aquinas and Dominican spirituality are often accused of placing too much emphasis on the human intellect (intellectualism) and neglecting the affective powers. It is true that for this tradition not only does the intellect guide the affective powers, but also the affective powers have as their goal the more perfect operation of the intellect. Nevertheless, it is not true that the Dominican tradition neglects the faculty of the will, its freedom, and its dynamism of love, nor the lower affective powers of the emotions. The Renaissance reformer

Giovanni Dominici, O.P., shows the intimate relation of intellectuality and affectivity when he writes:[18]

> Because we journey in the present life by faith and see only as in an obscure and clouded mirror, the intellectual power does not seem to suffice of itself, if it is not informed by its granddaughter love. Charity is born of the knowledge of God which shows him so good, beneficial and delightful that it could only bring it about that the will, irradiated by such a light, comes to love him. In the same degree that love increases so knowledge is more clear and faith more firm and stable. But if love is then so great that it is reflected back on the intelligence it makes it impossible for the intelligence to see anything but God, because the intelligence cannot represent to itself anything it does not see. Thus the spirit can not grow sad but rejoices always, even if the sensibility suffers some pain. I have seen a ray of the sun focused by a mirror get hot and enkindle a fire, although its ordinary effect is not to burn but to illuminate. Just so, one may say, the intelligence when it strikes a pure will rebounds and reflects the act of the will on the intelligence itself so that it enkindles the flame of love and burns away all the interior weaknesses of the soul, setting them ablaze like torches that cry out "O sweet love; O God who is love! Love melt my heart so that I cannot live without love."

Modern psychotherapy deals with these problems of the inner imaginative and affective life by enabling a client to verbalize or otherwise symbolically express these memories and subconscious confusions and frustrated feelings so as to become fully conscious of them and able to relate them to the person's real situation in life and thus to bring them under free control. Today we are able to correct some malfunctions of the brain and nervous system by drugs and even by surgery so as to restore the sufferer's normal psychological capacities at the animal level. Similarly, through psychotherapy we can reeducate the person to deal with their inner senses and feelings in a more realistic and free manner.

The Ethical Dimension of the Human Person

As spiritual directors probe deeper into the inner life of those they guide, they cannot avoid that level of human behavior which is sometimes revealed only to the confessor, the level of moral responsibility, the level of good and sinful actions. Then the hard questions must be asked: *"Are you being truthful with me?* Have you followed your conscience, or have you sinned and are making excuses, trying to fool yourself and deny your responsibility for your troubles by blaming God or others?" It is the painful level of confrontation.

Only when a person is sufficiently physiologically and psychologically normal with a considerable area of real freedom, in her or his life can the question of ethics or morality fully emerge. Ethical problems belong to the sphere of the ego where persons consider possible means to attain the ends or goals to which they have committed themselves. Such problems are similar to technical problems in which one tries to determine the best means to produce a desired result—to reach a predetermined goal; but they differ from technical problems in that the goals are not particular ones which we are simply free to aim at or not, but are the goals necessary to a truly satisfactory human life. Or to put it in a different way, the goals of technological decisions are conditional, those of ethical or moral decisions are unconditional.

Thus if I want to build a house, I must decide whether to use wood, stone, or bricks; but I may not want to build a house, so my decision is only conditional. But since I want to be happy, I must choose among different life-styles, some of which lead to happiness and some to self-destruction, and I *must make a decision*. Thus, moral decisions are unconditional; they must be made, because I cannot seek another goal than happiness.

The principal reason that moral decisions are difficult is our human capacity to deceive ourselves, to pretend to ourselves that some immediate satisfaction will bring us happiness, when in fact our reason tells us (if only we will use it), that this immediate satisfaction in the long run will prevent us from attaining true satisfaction in life. The Thomistic view of morality holds that morality is simply acting according to reason, i.e., according to the reality of what makes for true human happiness and what does not. It has always opposed the common view (voluntarism or legalism), which came to dominate much Catholic moral theology after the Council of Trent, that immorality is simply breaking the laws of God or human society.

The reason it is wrong to break God's law or those of society, is not because of the arbitrary will of authority, whether that of human society or even of God, but rather God's laws give us a realistic understanding of what is really for our happiness and what is not, and so do society's laws if they are conformed to God's laws. In short, something is moral or immoral not because authority wills it to be so, but genuine authority, and supremely God, wills it to be moral or immoral because it *is* so in realistic fact.

Because we can so easily fool ourselves about what is good and bad for us, and because we live in a society where there are many voices trying to fool us, and because we often lack, especially when we are young, sufficient experience for our reason to show us the truth, our moral judgments require help from the experience of society expressed in its laws, from experienced counselors, and above all from the Holy Spirit of God speaking through the church. But we cannot escape personal responsibility for choosing our counselors well and honestly applying what they tell us to the unique situations of our lives.

There is a special emphasis in the moral teaching of Aquinas, which goes back to Augustine and is found in such early Dominican works as the *Summa of Virtues and Vices* of Guillaume Peyraut, on our need to develop the virtues, i.e., the special skills in dealing with certain types of problems which constitute a good character, and avoiding the formation of vices which constitute a bad character. A person without virtue can do the right thing, but is very likely also to do the wrong thing. Only by consistently doing the right thing do we acquire a virtue which gives our character stability, so that it actually becomes difficult for us to do what is wrong; just as by repeatedly doing the wrong thing we acquire a vice that strongly inclines us to keep doing that wrong. To become Christ-like, therefore, is to acquire the virtues which Jesus had, since "a good tree cannot bear bad fruit, nor a rotten tree good fruit" (Mt 7:18).

Aquinas accepted the ancient scheme of the four cardinal virtues which correspond to the four most difficult life problems that we each have to meet: (1) We have to learn to refrain from immoderate pleasures (food, drugs, sex, etc.) which ruin our health or cause us to become irresponsible (Temperance or Moderation); (2) We have to learn to endure hardships and undergo risks in order to do what we know is right (Fortitude or Courage); (3) We have to respect the rights of other persons, and not merely regard our own interests (Justice or Righteousness); (4) We have to use our reason well in making moral decisions in order not to fool ourselves or allow ourselves to be fooled (Prudence or Practical Wisdom).

Ethical problems are, of course, part of the role of the confessor who must be trained in moral theology, but they are not the specific role of spiritual directors, although they must confront evident moral failures and aberrations in those they guide. What then is the spiritual director's specific task?

The Spiritual Dimension of the Human Person

It is at the deepest stage of spiritual direction, when it becomes truly spiritual healing, and not merely psychotherapy or moral advice, that one finally has to ask the question: *What really counts in your life? What are you really living for?*

We have just seen that according to Aquinas ethical decision has to do with using our reason in choosing the right means to the true goals of human life. The specific role of the spiritual director is to raise questions, not about the means to attain the goals of life, but about commitment to these goals. But how do we know what these true goals are? Aquinas argues that our human intelligence has two aspects: first of all it is an intelligence, an ability to have insight into reality; second it is reason.

God knows all things directly and immediately because he creates them. He is Pure Intelligence, Pure Insight and has no need of reasoning to complete his perfect knowledge. The created intelligences we call angels also have a direct insight into reality and do not require reason, but their insights are limited by the various degrees of intellectuality and the innate ideas with which they were created by God. The human being, however, as we have seen, has the very least possible kind of intelligence, one that is dependent on experiences gained through the body to know anything. Consequently, we are not able to gather many insights directly from experience, and those we have are very vague and general. That is why we must also use our intelligence to reason analytically about our experience in the light of such insights as we already possess. By reasoning we are able to analyze the details of our experience and gradually to develop our insights so as to make them much more specific and concrete. Thus, on first meeting a giraffe, my insight tells me that it is something alive, but only by considerable further observation and reasoning do I conclude that it is a mammal somewhat like an antelope, but with a long neck to eat leaves from high trees. Thus reasoning begins with insight, is at its service, and should end by producing a more perfect insight.

Yet the basis of our reasoning is such insights or first principles as we may have. Consequently, in ethical reasoning, we must always begin from our basic moral insight, which is simply "Do good and avoid evil," or to state it more accurately, as we have already explained, "Choose the reasonable means to attain true human happiness and avoid means that lead us from that goal." Thus our commitment to the true goal of human happiness lies very deep in our souls, not just at the level of reason, but at the level of insight, or first principles. This commitment, of course, is not just a matter of the intelligence, but also of the spiritual free will which follows on the intelligence but determines its final practical judgment that this is the goal that ought to be pursued.

While reasoned understandings are easy to verbalize and occur in the arena of the ego or consciousness, insights are at a higher (or deeper) level of the soul, the superconscious (not the superego of Freud which is for him part of the unconscious). Aquinas speaks of these respectively as the *ratio inferior* and the *ratio superior.* In the terminology of Dionysian mysticism the latter is the *apex mentis,* the top of the mind, or *scintillae animae* or *fünklein,* where the intelligence and the will meet in the act of total commitment. In the Bible this depth of the soul is often referred to as "the heart." Meister Eckhart goes even further and says,[19]

> But I say that it [beatitude] does not consist in either knowing or loving, but that there is that in the soul from which knowing and loving flow; that something does not know or love as do the powers of the soul. Whoever knows this knows in what blessedness consists.

> If a man will turn away from himself and from all created things, by so much will you be made one and blessed in the spark in the soul, which has never touched time or place. This spark rejects all created things, and wants nothing but its naked God, as he is in himself....I will say more, surprising though this is. I speak in all truth, truth that is eternal and enduring, that this same light is not content with the simple divine essence in its repose, as it neither

gives nor receives; but it wants to know the source of this essence, it wants to go into the simple ground, into the quiet desert, in which distinction never gazed, not the Father, nor the Son, nor the Holy Spirit. In the innermost part, where no one dwells, there is contentment for that light, and there it is more inward than it can be to itself, for this ground is a simple silence, in itself immovable, and by immobility all things are moved, all life is received by those who in themselves have rational being.

Transcendental Thomists like Karl Rahner have reformulated this in Kantian terms by distinguishing transcendental freedom and the fundamental option from categorial freedom and categorial decisions. The danger of this distinction, as pointed out in the recent encyclical of John Paul II, *Veritatis Splendor*, is so to dichotomize the two levels of consciousness as to conclude that one can remain committed to God at the deep level of the fundamental option, while at the same time committing serious sins at the more superficial, categorial level.

The truth in the fundamental option theory is to recognize (without necessarily committing oneself to Transcendentalism) that our deepest commitments, which are the first principles of our free decisions, lie at a deep level which is not easy to verbalize. Thomists, such as Ambrose Gardeil, O.P. and Jacques Maritain, have, therefore, spoken of such insights as "preconceptual" ("inchoatively conceptual" would be better, since all specifications of the intelligence are "conceptual") and explained them as based on "co-naturality." They are "co-natural" in the sense that the intelligence is naturally proportioned to perceive their truth immediately from experience, not mediately by reasoning.

Furthermore, as persons become formed in virtue, both intellectual and moral, they acquire, so to speak, a "second nature" which proportions them to more perfect insights. St. Paul, therefore, says of true Christians, "we have the mind of Christ." Thus, our fundamental practical insights at the level of the intelligence as such (*ratio superior*) are co-natural but only inchoatively conceptual and the fundamental option which follows on them shares in these characteristics.

It does not follow, however, that one can retain one's fundamental option for the true goals of human life and at the same time deliberately and freely commit serious moral wrongs. One can indeed commit venial wrongs and even objectively serious moral wrongs when one's full

freedom is not involved through ignorance, impulse or lack of deliberation, but a fully deliberate free choice to do something seriously wrong
goes right to the heart of one's fundamental option and switches it to
another false option, because it contradicts the true one. Thus, the traditional distinction between a mortal and a venial sin must be maintained; any fully deliberate and free choice to do something seriously
wrong (i.e., contradictory to the true goal of human life) is a mortal sin
which deprives the person of the life of grace and plunges them into
spiritual death from which only God's mercy can revive them.

But how is it possible for a person to choose to live for some other
goal in life than the true goal of human happiness; for example, to live
simply for physical pleasure, or for money, or power? We are *not* free
to choose anything else but happiness as our ultimate goal, because this
is determined in the very nature given us by God. Our intelligence
shows us what that happiness is in a general, vague way. It means the
integral satisfaction of all our basic needs, and the clear and more complete understanding we have of what our needs are, i.e., what human
nature is, the more evident it is what true happiness is.

Aquinas sums it up by saying that we can all recognize that we have
four basic kinds of needs that require to be harmoniously satisfied: (1)
the need for physical well-being, health; (2) the need for society with
other persons; (3) the need for the family without which society cannot
exist or continue; (4) the need for truth or meaning in life. He also
shows that while moderate physical pleasure is necessary for health, it
cannot be as such one of the essential goods, nor true happiness as he-
donists suppose, because it can in fact be destructive of happiness (as
for example the pleasure of drunkenness, drugs, or promiscuous sex).

Yet because of our human mode of knowing, at times one or the
other good may appear more attractive than what we realistically know
is our true happiness; therefore, it is possible for us freely and deliberately to choose it as an apparent happiness or what we know to be real
happiness. Thus the fundamental option of the sinner is to choose to be
what he really knows he is not, to be happy in a way that cannot really
make him happy. It is the choice of moral autonomy, to be a law-unto-
oneself, rather than to conform to the real law of one's own nature; to
be one's own creator, rather than to cooperate with one's Creator in his
creative work. Thus Eve and Adam yielded to the serpent's illusory
promise that they could be "like gods knowing what is good and what

is bad" (Gn 3:6). Their sin was not to want to be like God, for that is to be happy, but to choose to be "gods" who themselves decided what was to be "good" and "bad," rather than accept what God in his perfect wisdom would show them to be *really* good and *really* evil.

In view of this analysis of Aquinas, it becomes clear why the level of spiritual direction is to be distinguished from that of merely ethical direction. Ethical counselors presuppose that their client wishes to live a life according to reason, according to one's nature, committed to the true goals of human life. If they are not so committed, there is no point in counseling them, since they do not accept the first principles of morality. The object of moral counseling is to help the client determine the best means to these true goals to which they are already committed.

Spiritual counselors, on the other hand, must go deeper and raise the questions about whether the persons who seek their guidance are really committed to the goals to which they claim to be committed, or whether there is something false and hypocritical about this commitment. Or, to look at it from the client's point of view, we go to a spiritual director because we want to be a good person, but we realize that somehow in our hearts we are resistant to a full and genuine commitment to God and our true self, and we need to be delivered from these resistances. Thus the spiritual director's questions must always seek to help the client penetrate these delusions, this pride, and false claims to absolute autonomy, and to open up to God's grace.

The Human Person and Sexuality

A very delicate and today controversial dimension of human personality is sexuality and gender. Yet spiritual directors who out of fear of treading on some landmine, avoid questions about how their clients understand and live their sexuality, will be of little help to their spiritual growth, so fundamental is this factor to human personality. The question must be asked, *How does being a woman (or a man) affect your life and your relation to God?*

As I have indicated in our first chapter, the Dominican family from the first has included both women and men, and women have been very important in the development of its tradition of spirituality. St. Catherine of Siena can rightly be considered its second founder, and its only church doctor so designated especially by reason of her spiritual doctrine. Yet St. Thomas Aquinas, its chief theologian, is cited by many in the women's movement as supremely sexist in his views on the differences between men and women.

I do not intend here to defend Aquinas on this point. He was a man of his time and insensitive to the issues of sexism with which we are trying to deal at present. Yet Aquinas firmly held that male and female human persons are as persons created in the image of God and equally human, equally members of the human community. That is for St. Thomas the fundamental principle in understanding their relationship, and everything else he says must be interpreted in view of that principle, which he certainly never intended to contradict.[20]

Yet if all human persons are essentially alike and form one single human community of equal persons why do they divide into two sexes? This division is not essential but "accidental," as is, for example, the division of humans into different races or different temperaments. But it is, nevertheless, a natural division, because it has a natural purpose necessary to the human species, namely, for its reproduction. Human gender is primarily a difference in the body, but, since for Aquinas who was no Platonic or Cartesian dualist, the soul is the form of the body and proportioned to it, this bodily difference conditions the soul, so that men and women differ not only in body but also in soul, although this difference is a modal not a specific difference, i.e., it is not due to a specific difference of form but to the relation (proportion) of the form to the individual matter, just as are individual differences within each of the sexes.

Naturally speaking, the human species is divided equally into male and female, so that every human can find a partner and form a marriage, and if there had been no fall into sin, naturally all persons would have married. It is the disordered, eschatological condition of fallen human society that makes it reasonable that now some should choose to be celibate in order to be free of domestic entanglements and enabled to devote themselves more fully to eternal concerns. Hence the relation between man and woman is first that of equality in personhood, but second and in subordination to their personal equality a relation of functional complementarity, i.e., each contributes to the other what is lacking in the other, not as if one were more a person than the other, but in order that as equally persons they might jointly transmit life to other new persons.

Some feminists object to this term "complementarity" because it seems to imply that woman is incomplete without man. They prefer the term "mutuality." But this misses the point that "complementarity" equally implies that a man is incomplete without woman. Moreover, a "complementary" relation is also one of "mutuality" but a mutuality between equals who are also different. Moreover, this complementarity should not be understood to deny to women the capacity to develop the more masculine side of their personalities, nor of men to develop the more feminine side of their personalities. Both genders approach the same fullness of human personhood but from somewhat different starting points. Thus, not to acknowledge sexual difference within equality and mutuality, is to deny the great significance of human sexuality, and thus block our understanding of its influence on spiritual development.

The differentiation of the sexes must, therefore, be understood in relation to the family institution for which it was designed, a monogamous family of woman and man, permanently committed to each other in love and in care for their children, who because of the long development required of the complex human person, require a long development of body and character. All members of such a family are equal as persons, but they have different roles to play. The children are subordinate to the parents, yet the parents care for the children for the children's sake, and not as their possessions. The husband is obliged to care for his wife and children because without his wife he can never complete his own personhood as a man or have a family, and the wife differs from the husband not as a person, since in that she is his equal, but as one who cannot have a family without a husband, nor adequately care for her family without his care. Yet the fullness of human personhood for the woman as for the man is not realized in the narrow circle of the family, but in the wider community for which family living is only a preparation, although a necessary one.

If, then, we attempt to say how man and woman differ from each other and complement each other, the best answer seems to be that sexually they are fitted body and soul to be a father or mother in the structure of a family. No doubt these differences can be expressed in different ways in human culture at different times and places, but these cultural forms must respect the basic structure of the family and its common good if they are to meet the needs of all. In our time the general limitation of married women to domestic life which was unavoidable in medieval society has been overcome. Thus, on Thomistic principles, we can conclude that in modern society, all types of careers are open to women equally with men, providing that they are compatible with their responsibilities of motherhood, but men too must first fulfill their family responsibilities before they devote themselves to other concerns.

Finally, it should be emphasized that biological motherhood and fatherhood are as such less significant than the spiritual motherhood and fatherhood which persons learn through loving and educating their children and which they then extend to the service of others in society beyond the domestic limits. Dedicated celibates also share in this spiritual parentage. As St. Paul said of himself to the Corinthians, "I became your father in Christ Jesus through the gospel (1 Cor 4:15)." Without the gift of sexuality this spiritual self-giving would be difficult for fleshly human beings to attain. Spiritual direction is an especially beautiful example of such spiritual parentage. The woman director and the man director will each bring to it special but not identical gifts.

Spiritual counselors, therefore, should first of all recognize their own androcentric or gynocentric perspective, with both its opportunities and its limitations. Then, while treating men and women clients equally as persons, directors should take into account how the modal, but non-essential differences of being women or men and the life experiences these entail affect their spiritual development and in particular their relation to God. The problems in spiritual growth that women and men meet have much in common, but also raise questions peculiar to each.

The Human Person as Individual and as Communitarian

Even when we have begun to understand someone as a human person, we need to ask the question, *How do you as a unique person relate to the communities in which you live, your family, your religious community, your fellow workers, the community you serve, the state, the nation, the world community?*

One of the advantages of the origin of the human person through sexual reproduction is that the combination of genetic traits from two parents insures a great variation in the bodily characteristics of persons and hence of the uniqueness of the souls which God creates for such varied bodies. Even identical twins, we now know, are not absolutely identical in inheritance. According to Aquinas no two angels are the same species, because they are pure forms. Yet this inequality of the angelic persons, which in their case, unlike for us, is specific and not merely accidental, does not prevent them from forming a community. Instead, as St. Thomas explains, the hierarchy of the angles form a marvelously united community of knowledge and love, since by reason of their different gifts each angel contributes to the common good and each receives from it.

Human beings, unlike angelic persons, can be of one species and form a community of personally equal members precisely because they are bodily beings. But there is an even profounder reason for the uniqueness of each human person, namely that the spiritual soul of the human person cannot be produced by the parents or by any material process, but has to be created immediately out of nothing by God for the body produced by God through the parents. Thus from the first moment of its existence each human person stands in direct and immediate relation to its creator as person-to-person, I to Thou.

The human being is a person from the first moment of its conception. While Aristotle and Aquinas thought that the embryo became a person only one or two months after conception because the matter out of which it was formed was at first relatively unformed and it took some time for the male seed remaining in the womb to form it to the point when it was prepared for the soul, modern biology has shown that the ovum is already highly organized and requires no further action than fertilization by the male parent to develop.

Since the embryo is a unique combination of traits which are unified in a single substance, each individual is said to have a temperament (more or less harmonious mixture), which like the difference of gender, is modal and non-essential. As a convenient broad classification of temperaments, Aquinas refers to the fourfold types mentioned commonly by ancient characterologists, the phlegmatic person who reacts slowly to experiences and retains little from them; the mercurial person who reacts quickly but retains little; the choleric who reacts quickly and retains much; the melancholic who reacts slowly but retains much. These temperaments were thought to correspond to different balances of "humors" (we would say "hormones") in the physiology of the body. Today, many similar classifications have been proposed, such as those of Carl Gustav Jung (extrovert vs. introvert, and the fourfold *mandala* of Thought vs. Feeling, Intuition vs. Sensation), and the elaborate diagram, dubiously claimed to be of Sufi origin, the "Enneagram." For counselors these typologies have some suggestive use in trying to understand individual differences, but none of them seem to be really scientific. The difficulty of a director coming to a fair and balanced understanding of individual differences is illustrated by the following passage from Venturino de Bergamo:[21]

> There are some so perverse, that they judge ill of everything. For they say that if someone studies, he is a dreamer, if he practices humility that he is a hypocrite; if he recreates that he is a glutton; if he is religious that he is simple-minded; if he is sociable, that he is singular; if he is given to silence and peace that he is deceitful; if he corrects others, that he is presumptuous; if he gives himself to vigils and prayer, that he is indiscrete; if he takes a nap, that he is a sleepy head; if he gives himself to preaching and the salvation of others, he is seeking praise; if he ceases to do so, that he is negligent and remiss; if he is thankful that he is a flatterer; if he fails to praise others that he is proud.

Although the individual is a person from conception, the natural capacities which flow from this personhood require a long development through the nine months of pregnancy, infancy, childhood, adolescence, maturity, old age. Erik Erikson and others have studied these developmental phases in detail. While the time within the family undoubtedly lays the basis of character, of moral and intellectual development, learning goes on throughout human life until intelligence degenerates and is lost.

The natural institution of the permanent monogamous family as necessary for the generation and education of children establishes the essentially social or communitarian nature of human persons, but does not complete it. We need to be generated and educated in the family because we are bodily beings, but the family is not sufficient to supply all our bodily or other needs, so we need the larger societies of the tribe, the nation, the state, or ultimately global society. But we also need community, not merely because we have needs based on our bodily existence, but also from our capacity as spiritual beings to communicate with other spirits. Because we are intelligent persons we want to know all things, and especially those highest in the scale of being, and these are other persons. In knowing other persons we find them the most lovable of all things and seek to form friendships with them in community. Those persons that are directly accessible to us are human persons, but we also want to enter into personal relationships with God and with other created intelligences (angels, Martians) if there are such beings. As the German Dominican apologist Albert Weiss, O.P. wrote:[22]

> Solitude cannot be too highly recommended to Christians, but only under the guidance of the Church; in any other case it may prove their ruin, as St. Basil the Great said in his *Longer Rule*, n.7). We humans need companionship: it is not good for us to be alone. Whatever we do apart from the society to which we belong, that we do for ourselves personally, but not for God who made us members of that society. Christ holds as his own all who are living members of his body, the Church, but those who sever themselves from this Church cut themselves off from life.

Thus, in Aquinas' list of the four basic goods of health, reproduction, society, and knowledge, the supreme good is knowledge, but principally the knowledge and love of other persons. It is also in this mutual knowledge of persons that the highest good of society consists. Health and reproduction are of value primarily because without health and reproduction there could be no society nor the common pursuit of knowledge.

Aquinas believed that although the structure of the familial society is determined naturally by the requirements of reproduction, larger societies have no naturally determined form, but are human constructs, created to meet particular historical circumstances. In most circumstances Aquinas thought (as did many Dominican writers such as Savonarola, Vitoria, and Bartolomé de las Casas) that the best form of government will be a republic which serves the common good by an appropriate mixture and balance of the democratic, aristocratic, and monarchical principles.

Conclusion

The four levels of the human person, as Aquinas has analyzed them, are generally recognized in all strands of the Dominican tradition. They are very clear, for example, in the writings of Catherine of Siena, not so clear in Eckhart who emphasizes the spiritual level almost to the exclusion of the others, yet does not exclude them. The spiritual director is concerned chiefly with the deepest of these levels, the level of ultimate commitment, but must take them all into account, while being quick to refer to other experts serious problems at the other three levels. The director who finds problems of environmental situation will refer the client to an ecologist, problems of physical health to a physician, problems of psychological health to the psychotherapists, problems of ethical conduct to the moralist.

St. Teresa of Avila advised a young nun who was having visions after excessive fasting to "eat some beef-steak," and Aquinas, I believe, would have approved of this counsel. Some of the practices of the saints raise questions today as to whether their directors sufficiently appreciated this principle. For example, when we read what Bl. Raymund of Capua tells us about St. Catherine's inability to eat, we cannot help but wonder whether this was miraculous or simply an unrecognized case of anorexia nervosa (motivated, however, by very different notions than modern ideas of self-worth based on being stylishly thin). With better modern ecological, physical and psychological knowledge we are in a better position to recognize some of these factors, although, it must be confessed, our ethical and spiritual insight actually seems to have deteriorated.

Above all we must recognize the essentially communitarian nature of human personhood. The kind of community we need is one that exists for the good of its members each of whom is unique in temperament and talents. We humans develop best in permanent monogamous families where man and wife play complementary roles and in a society so constructed that it provides not only a good physical environment and physical and psychological health, but which also enables its members to mutually search to understand the cosmos of which we are a part, to know and love each other, and above all, to know and love the triune God. Yet the families and societies in which we have grown up are tragically distorted by sin and fall far short of giving us all the help we need. Hence the spiritual counselor, while recognizing the individuality of each client, must always try to understand each one in terms of family background and social situations.

Thus, if we ask what is the special Dominican contribution to spirituality, the answer seems to be that it bears witness that the deepest, although often hidden, yearning of every human person is to enter into the community of truth where alone true love can flourish, the community of the three persons who are truth itself. St. Albert the Great, commenting on John 8:31–32, "The truth will set you free," wrote:[23]

> Because the word of the Lord is the truth it frees us from the compulsion and bondage of a passing world; because it is the word of grace, it frees us from the slavery of guilt and sin; because, finally, it is the word of the all powerful God, it frees us from the slavery of misery. The first gives freedom to our nature, the second gives us the freedom of grace, the third the freedom of glory.

And St. Catherine of Siena prayed;[24]

> Truth! Truth! And who am I that you give me your truth? I am the one who is not. It is your truth then that does and speaks and accomplishes all things, because I am not. It is your truth that offers truth and with your truth I speak the truth. Your eternal truth offers the truth in different ways to different people. Nor is your truth separate from you: in fact, you *are* Truth. You Godhead eternal, God's Son, came from the Father to fulfill the eternal Father's truth. No one can possess truth except from you, Truth. And those who want to possess your truth must have *all* of your truth; in no other way can they possess the truth which cannot be less than complete.

Chapter 3

Graced in Jesus Christ

Nature and Grace

Henri de Lubac has eloquently protested against the post-Tridentine theologians who made, or seemed to make, grace a second nature imposed on the first in the manner of the second-story of a house, an error he called *extrinsicism*.[25] He maintained, rightly enough, that no such extrinsicism is to be found in the church fathers nor even in St. Thomas Aquinas. In proof of this last point he cited Aquinas' thesis that humans have a "natural desire for the beatific vision." Hence, de Lubac concluded, we ought to deny that the human person has any other ultimate end than the beatific vision, i.e., there is no "natural end" of the human person. How explain then, the Catholic dogma that we are destined to the glory of the beatific vision only by grace and not by nature? De Lubac's reply, today accepted by many theologians, even conservative ones, is that although we have a natural desire for the beatific vision as our sole end, nevertheless we are utterly unable to obtain it without the help of supernatural grace.

In the metaphysics of St. Thomas, however, this explanation contradicts a fundamental principle: (a) Every nature has an end proportionate to it, as its "cause of causes"; (b) but there is no proportion between finite human nature and the infinity of God attained in the beatific vision. As for the passages in which Aquinas speaks of a "natural desire for the beatific vision," these occur in apologetic arguments whose purpose is to refute arguments against the possibility of the beatific vision. All that Aquinas seeks to establish is that all spiritual creatures desire to know all of Reality and hence to know the essence of God, if that is possible. Yet natural reason cannot show that such a knowledge of God by a creature is possible. Only revelation can guarantee this, since God has promised such a vision to those who believe in him and love him.

It is essential for a Thomistic understanding of the relation of grace to nature to see that, like St. Paul, Aquinas always maximizes the infinite difference between nature and grace. Martin Heidegger, perhaps the most influential philosopher of our times, has accused theologians of "onto-theology," by which he means the error of treating God as simply one "Being" among many "beings" even if the first and greatest of the many. This, for Heidegger, is to be "forgetful of Being, i.e., of the "difference" between Being and beings. It would be better to say, as the Pesudo-Dionysius did, that God is the "Being Beyond Being."

Heidegger's accusation is important, but it does not fit Aquinas. Aquinas held for the absolute, infinite "Otherness" of God from creatures and formulated it by saying that in creatures their acts of existence are really distinct from their essences, so that they are contingent and could just as well not be as be, while God is the I AM , whose very essence is to be. Hence he is the Source and Ground of all other beings, while being utterly other than and independent of them. St. Catherine of Siena, unlettered in metaphysics, had from God the insight that "You are the one who is not, I am the One Who IS."

Eckhart seems to contradict this when he says, "If I did not exist, God would not exist," but when we interpret this paradoxical saying in the light of his Platonic metaphysics it turns out to mean: "My true existence is not in my temporal self but in the eternal idea of myself by which God has created and sustains me in that existence and to which I will perfectly conform only when I am finally perfectly united to God; hence if God's idea of me did not exist I would not exist, but neither would God, since God's ideas and God are identical." Thus Eckhart agrees with Catherine, but at the expense of denying to creatures any proper existence of their own, which is not what Catherine, raised in the Thomistic tradition, must have meant. For St. Thomas, creation really and truly gives to the creature an existence which is a participation in God's existence but which God has truly given to it as its very own. To deny this is to deny the doctrine of free creation by God and God's infinite power and generosity as creator.

Yet we must grant to de Lubac that the term "nature" is only analogously applied to persons and to non-personal things. The nature of non-personal substances is "determined to one." It is that by which a thing, a chemical or an organism, behaves in a determinant, non-free manner. But a person is an intelligent and free substance, and to be intelligent is, according to Aristotle, to be somehow all that is, i.e., to be open to all Reality, including, therefore, the Divine Reality as it actually is. Human nature is personal and hence intelligent, and therefore it has as its natural end to know all reality insofar as it has the power to do so. But every created intelligence is limited, and of all created intelligences, human intelligence, dependent as it is on its body to know anything, is the most limited.

What are the limits of the human intelligence, according to Aquinas? Since it derives all its information from its bodily senses, its proper object is the essences of material things, and hence the whole physical cosmos is open to its discovery, although this exploration is difficult and will never be exhaustive. We quickly learn, however, from the changing and contingent character of the world and its cosmic order that the universe is not ultimately self-explanatory, that it must have as its first cause, a Being who is not a cause nor even a "being" in a physical sense, not a part of nature, but utterly other than its creation. Furthermore, by comparison of our own bodily being with other bodily beings, we come to realize that our own intelligence, our capability of scientific thought and technological invention, and our ability to communicate with other persons show that we are not merely bodily beings, but have spiritual intelligences dependent on our bodies to learn anything.

Hence, from the analogy of our own selves as intelligent, free persons, capable of morality, we come to know that the first cause is personal, the all-knowing and all-loving. Furthermore, we become convinced that, since we are the least possible of created intelligences, the variety, order and grandeur of the physical cosmos implies also a still greater range of created intelligences, superior to ourselves, called "angels" in the Bible, yet who are only creatures just as we are. Therefore, the more our human knowledge of the cosmos increases, the deeper grows our knowledge of ourselves in relation to the cosmos and in distinction from it, and the deeper we know ourselves, the truer our analogical knowledge of God becomes. Yet that knowledge of God will naturally always be limited by our creaturely way of knowing God from creatures rather than in God's own person.

God, however, has freely chosen, without any claim on the part of creatures, to invite those creatures who are persons, intelligent and free, and hence ends in themselves, to share in God's very own inner life, to know God as God really is in the Divine Self, and not merely in God's effects in creation, that is, we graciously are called to the "beatific vision" which will make us blessed, blissful, happy beyond all human limitations.

Therefore, God reveals the Divine Self to us by giving us the supernatural gifts of faith and of love, and the sure hope that faith will eventually brighten into the glory of vision and love, exceeding what faith can know, in perfect union with God. This invitation to union with God as God is, beyond all the limits of our nature, knowledge, and freedom, and the power to actually respond to it in faith, hope, and love is what we call grace (gift), precisely because it is utterly free on God's part, and in no way required by our own nature.

Yet it is intrinsic not extrinsic to our nature, because God as our creator and the very source of our being, is "closer to us than we are close to ourselves" (in the words of St. Augustine, which Aquinas quotes) and his grace penetrates to the very depths of our being transforming it in every element of our nature, body and soul. It is truly, in the words of St. Paul, "a new creation," a "rebirth."

In keeping with Aquinas' favorite saying, "Grace perfects nature," this transformation by grace is so utterly intrinsic that it destroys nothing of our human nature, but only its distortion by sin. Because we remain completely human we still must seek our natural end of being perfectly human, but through God's invitation and the power of his grace, this natural goal has become for us only a phase of the far longer journey to the Trinity. As Jesus is truly human, truly God, without his humanity being monophysically confused with or absorbed into his divinity, so the perfection of our human nature, freed by grace from sin, is not confused with or absorbed into our deification by grace. We remain our human selves, yet every fiber of our being is being transformed so as to make us adopted daughters and sons of God.

Fundamental, therefore, to all Christian spiritual direction, is to enable the client to grow ever more in the appreciation of the generous love of God in inviting us to union with God and the marvelous dignity that this confers on every human creature, no matter what their defects may be. Our humanity is restored to what it was created to be, but it is also so transformed that we share in the very life of the Trinity.

Created in God's Image and Likeness

Aquinas considered the theory, which some Greek philosophers had proposed as a possibility, that human beings have evolved from lower forms of life, but he rejected this idea because in his time there was no reliable evidence of any such biological evolution. He was also aware that the biblical account of creation was capable of a figurative as well as a literal interpretation, but preferred the latter on the general hermeneutical principle that language should be understood literally unless there is good reason to interpret it otherwise. Thus the Dominican tradition has been open to evidence both for biological evolution and for a critical interpretation of Genesis that would permit their reconciliation. At the beginning of this century, even before the publications of Teilhard de Chardin, the important Dominican spiritual writer, the Ven. Juan Arintero, sought to incorporate the theory of evolution into a spiritual theology. This move has also been supported by the historical biblical criticism in whose development another Dominican, M.-J. Lagrange, founder of the Ecole Biblique in Jerusalem, played so leading a part.

Today Catholic theologians are generally in agreement that there is no contradiction between a sound biological theory of evolution and a sound exegesis of Genesis. There is sufficient evidence both that human beings evolved from non-human primate animals and that the inspired author of Genesis did not intend to assert that humanity literally originated as he tells the tale, but only to present in story form certain basic facts about the human condition, namely, that we are created by God in his image, that we all belong to one human community by nature and descent, that God created us good by nature and in grace, and that we have lost this grace through the original sin of our first parents.

But what does the statement that "God created humanity in his own image" (Gn 1:27) or "image and likeness" (Gn 1:26) mean? According to Aquinas (I: q.93) the term "likeness" indicates that we, like all creatures, resemble our creator as all effects resemble their causes, but the term "image" indicates that we resemble God, not in some merely external manner, but in God's inner being as a personal God, for we, too, are persons. Furthermore, Aquinas suggests that although we are created in God's image, that image can be rendered more intensively similar by our acquisition of virtues. It may be, therefore, that the Bible, by using the terms "likeness" and "image," indicates this growth from a lesser to a greater similarity to God to which he has called us. This second interpretation was favored by many of the Eastern church fathers. Meister Eckhart speaks of this likeness to God in somewhat different language. He says: [26]

> When I preach, it is my wont to speak about detachment, and of how we should rid ourselves of self and all things. Secondly, that man should be informed back into the simple good which is God. Thirdly, that we should remember the great nobility God has put into the soul, so that man may come miraculously to God. Fourthly, of the purity of the divine nature, for the splendor of God's nature is unspeakable.

Thus, all human persons are copies of God, but this copy is found in the spiritual soul rather than in the body which as something material is, like all material creation, similar to God as an effect to its cause, but not as image but as a "vestige." (It should not be forgotten, however, that the body expresses or mirrors its soul). For Aquinas, this image of the Trinity in the soul is to be found in the fact that our intelligence and our free will proceed from the soul and terminate in our knowledge and love of ourselves by which we are united to ourselves, just as in God the Father's Son or Word and the Father's Spirit or Love proceed from him and unite him to himself in knowledge and love in one single Godhead. Because God knows and loves himself with a perfect knowledge and love, he is free to know and love his creation and seek to draw them into community with himself, so when we learn to know and love ourself without illusion and with an unselfish love like God's, we will be able to know and love all God's creatures as he loves them, and to know God by his own light and love him by his own heart. As the Trinity is a communion of life, of truth, and of love, so God has created each one of us to be within our souls communions of life, truth, and love that we seek to share with one another.

This image of God, therefore, is implanted in our human nature, but it is brought to perfection ("likeness" in the intensive sense) only by grace, by "participation in the divine nature" (2 Pt 1:4). Some of the medieval theologians, St. Bonaventure for one, thought Adam and Eve were created as purely natural beings, and then were later endowed with grace; but Aquinas held that we were created from the beginning with a nature transformed by grace. The effect of original sin, therefore, was primarily that our first parents lost this original blessing of grace, both for themselves and for all their descendants to whom they were intended by God to pass it on as an inheritance.

Fallen Human Nature

In chapter 5, we will discuss more fully the meaning of "the Fall" and "original sin" and what it has done to the image of God in us. Here it suffices to say that, for Aquinas the fall has deprived the whole human race of grace and hence of the splendid "image and likeness" of which Genesis speaks, but that it has not destroyed the natural image, since that is our very nature without which we could not even exist. Even the evil angels retain their natural likeness to God. This is why the Dominican tradition has never been tempted into the pessimistic Protestant notion of the fall as the "total corruption" of human nature, nor even the Jansenist exaggerations of the effect of the fall.

Yet this does not mean that our human nature is now the same as it might have been if God had created us, as he might have done (*pace* de Lubac, simply as natural beings untransformed by grace. We still have our whole human nature, but it is a "wounded nature." In what, then, does this "woundedness" or "brokenness" consist? Thomists explain it this way: The "integrity" of human nature consists in the harmonious unity of its parts in relation to the goal or end to which human nature tends. If we had been created without grace that goal would be purely natural, the harmonious fulfillment of the needs of our nature; but since God subordinated that natural goal to the higher goal of a share in his own life by grace, the integrating and unifying principle for us from the beginning was not merely the goal of nature but the goal of grace. Though sin has deprived us of grace, yet God has not ceased to invite us to share his life. We are born without an attraction to that goal, yet neither can we be satisfied to seek a merely natural end which is meaningless without the higher goal to which it is subordinate.

Thus we sinners are born without any goal that could unify our nature except the illusory goals we choose for ourselves, principally our own autonomy which can never unify a nature that is driven to transcend itself through knowledge and love of the ideal good. The wounds of sin, therefore, do not deprive us of any of our natural human powers, but only of the harmony between these powers, so that we find ourselves in sinful conflict with ourselves, "a law of the members warring against the law of the spirit" as St. Paul expresses it (Rm 7:23). As an orchestra without a conductor gets out of tune and time and produces only noise, yet all the players are still there playing, so does the sinful human person who has lost the true goal in life that would have kept his or her life together. Spiritual directors, therefore, must respect the humanity of those they seek to help, and remember that their task is to help them to be truly converted to the true goals of life for which God created and called them, so that they may, in the slang phrase, "get it all together."

Grace and Free Will

The doctrine that without grace the sinner cannot be converted and move toward his true goal in life, which is so clear in the Epistles of St. Paul, on which Aquinas wrote profound commentaries, which if they had been known to Luther might well have supplied him with more balanced answers to the questions that tormented him and not the one-sided *sola fides, sola gratia* that split the church in the Reformation. How is it possible to reconcile our need for grace with our apparent power of free choice? And if the sinner has no free choice how can God blame him for sinning? Aquinas gave a profound answer to such questions, and this answer was developed extensively by such Thomists as Domingo Bañez, Tomas de Lemos and others in the famous, but inconclusive "Commission on Grace" (*Congregatio de Auxiliis*) set up by Pope Clement VIII and continued under his two successors.

A Jesuit theologian, Luis de Molina (d. 1600), had proposed the view that we can reconcile the fact of human free choice with the doctrine that God knows the future and hence who will gain heaven and who will go to hell, by supposing that between God's foreknowledge of whom he will reward with heaven and whom he will punish with hell, and his foreknowledge of who will in fact deserve heaven by doing good and who will deserve hell by doing evil, God has a third kind of knowledge (*scientia media*, middle knowledge) of what each person will do if placed in certain circumstances. Hence, since through this middle knowledge God knows who will actually do good and who will actually do evil of their own free will in certain circumstances, and he also knows what these circumstances will be, he also foreknows who will do good and deserve heaven and who will do evil and deserve hell, without God himself in any way being the cause of their choosing one or the other, except that those who do good do so by cooperating with God's grace. The intention of Molina and his disciples was, of course, to refute the Calvinist view and the influence it had on Jansenists that God created some creatures for heaven and some for hell.

Thomists also, of course, absolutely rejected such Calvinistic and Jansenistic views, but they have always regarded the theory of the *scientia media* not only as an inadequate answer to Calvin, but as a theory which fell into the very error it was trying to answer, because it also amounted to a denial of free will, while at the same time undermining the absolute sovereignty of God and of grace. If God foreknows our free acts, because he knows how we will act if placed in certain circumstances, then such acts are not free. If on the other hand we can make an act of choice without all that it is good in that choice depending on the causality of God, then God is not God, i.e. the First Cause of all positive reality.

How then does the Dominican tradition reconcile God's universal causality and human freedom? For Thomists, God knows the whole history of the creation, from its beginning to its end, in the simultaneous Now of eternity, but he knows it because he causes every historical event. Yet he causes these events to happen in different ways. Natural events he causes to happen according to natural law, chance events to happen by the accidental coincidence of natural forces, and free events he causes to happen freely by elevating them to a participation in his own divine freedom, so that they are not determined by natural laws or accidental circumstances. How God is able to do this remains a mystery to us like the mystery of creation, but no contradiction can be found in claiming this to be possible for the first cause, although it is contradictory for finite causes to be able to do so. Thus Jesus' words, "Without me you can do nothing" (Jn 15:5) are literally true. When we freely perform any act, we must attribute all that is positively good in it to God, but whatever is evil in it must be attributed to ourselves.

Is sin, then, also caused by the first cause? St. Thomas answers by pointing out that a sinful act must have some goodness in it, insofar as it is a positive reality (for example, an act of murder can be performed in a clever, skillful, way), but it is a sin because it falls short of what is required by God for our good (thus the murderer should have used his cleverness and skill not to kill but to help his neighbor). Thus God as first cause is cause of all that is positive in every human act, but we as sinners are the defective causes of what is lacking in our sinful acts. Non-being has no cause except non-being. But all being has God as its first cause, and our good acts in their free goodness are therefore, primarily caused by him, secondarily by ourselves.

This conception of the relation of grace and free will, profound and mysterious as it is, nevertheless, leads to trust in God and away from claims to absolute autonomy on our part. Yet it gives to us responsibility for our acts and confidence that we can do right with the unfailing help of God. Of course we may be tempted to say, "Maybe God knows that I will ultimately fall into mortal sin before death and go to hell. What then is the use even trying?" but the answer to this is the Christian virtue of hope with its perfect assurance, that will be discussed in chapter 7.

It is fundamental for spiritual direction to encourage those they guide to keep to the fore in their meditations their absolute dependence on the help of God, and the conviction that "God, [is] our savior, who wills everyone to be saved and to come to the knowledge of the truth." (1 Tm 2:4). Hence, prayer to God for his help is the basis of all Christian life. As St. Antoninus of Florence said: [27]

> You ought not to doubt of the grace of God; for the least degree of grace is sufficient to resist every temptation and trial. And if after confession the sinner receives communion, he receives great strength [to resist sin], especially because he becomes a sharer in all the good works that are done in the Church.

Christian Perfection

In the Sermon on the Mount Jesus says, "Be perfect, just as your heavenly Father is perfect" (Mt 5:48). Surely, this was not to encourage the neurosis psychologists call "perfectionism," the obsession with details and excessive guilt over minor failings, nor the perfectionism that is a self-centered and self-righteous concern only with one's superiority to others, an anxiety to deny every weakness. What Jesus meant by being "perfect" was being complete, attaining the true goal of our lives, just as God is at the goal of the dynamism of all things, indeed is that very goal.

We certainly are never complete Christians in this life. Our journey to perfection lies beyond this life in our final union with God, but we have all experienced in getting ready for a journey that once we finally get on the airplane and it ascends and takes aim at where we are going, we feel in a sense that the journey is safely on its way and is, in anticipation, already practically completed. So it is with the Christian perfection to which Jesus calls us. If we are headed in the right direction to the right goal and empowered by grace to reach it, we are on the way.

What is it that thus sets us on course and empowers us to move straight toward it? Aquinas, and all the classical writers on the spiritual life, although they have different views on many things, are agreed on this point—it is love, not any sort of love but what the New Testament calls *agape*, charity, the love of God above all things and our neighbor as ourself, which Jesus says is the greatest commandment. Thus, "Be perfect" means "Love God and your neighbor as yourself" nothing more and nothing less. The intellectualism which Aquinas especially contributed to the Dominican tradition, does not stand in the way of this emphasis on the primacy of love. As Vincent Contenson, O.P., wrote: [28]

> Thus the law of Christ is written not on tablets of stone but by the Holy Spirit in the heart. Therefore, my prayer to the God of my life will be from the heart. I will pray in the spirit, pray in the mind, sing psalms in the spirit, sing songs in the mind. I will give my heart to watching till the dawn for the Lord who made me. I will not weary myself in paging over my books, but I will turn inward to my heart, that my heart may warm within me, that in my meditation a fire may be enkindled. I will not ascend the mountain to pray so as to be closer to God, because he who dwells in the heights, comes close to the humble when their hearts are converted. Therefore, I will descend, that I may ascend; or rather I will put down the risings in my heart and take my place there in the valley of tears.

Yet, in the Dominican tradition, real love always has its source and its goal in truth. Hence St. Catherine of Siena, echoing St. Paul (1 Cor 13), tells us in her *Dialogue* (c. 12) that when she prayed God to punish her for sins, he replied:

> I who am Truth have taught you now what you need to know to achieve and maintain the highest perfection. I have told you as well how sin and its penalty are atoned for in yourself and in your neighbors, reminding you that the pains you endure while in the mortal body are worth nothing in terms of atonement unless they are joined with loving charity, true contrition, and contempt for sin. But suffering so joined with charity atones not by virtue of any actual pain you may endure but by virtue of charity and sorrow for the sin you have committed. This charity is attained with the light of understanding, with a heart sincere and free gazing into me as its object—for I myself am this charity.

Thus in this life Christian perfection consists in growth in true love of God, of self, and of neighbor for God's sake. It is vital that the spiritual director constantly refer to this standard as the one by which the progress of the client is to be judged, and by no other standard. Extraordinary experiences and even extraordinary actions tell us nothing about the progress of the Christian, but only the evidence of genuine love. Later we will discuss what is true Christian love and what is counterfeit. This true love is, of course, made possible for us only by God's grace, since it is a participation in God's love for us. "We love because He first loved us" (1 Jn 4:19).

St. Catherine de Ricci, O.P., replying to a letter of Sister Maria Maddalen Strozzi asking guidance in finding "a true way to serve our Bridegroom" and for a "summa of the entire spiritual life" answered her that: [29]

> There are three points which make up the sum of Christian perfection (1) "To love God alone," for pure love of him as his goodness is pure; (2) "To look only for his glory...both as to ourselves and to others so that they may love and honour God because of us...(3) To remain always at God's disposal.

And she concludes by saying that the reason for all this is that "God can't go wrong [because he is] supremely good, lovable and health-giving."

In order to keep before the beginner a balanced view of what
Christian perfection is, an important means is well-chosen spiritual
reading, and a spiritual director should be of special help in its selection. Fr. Victorino Osende, O.P., a contemporary Spanish writer on spirituality says: [30]

> It would be the greatest imprudence to take for our spiritual read-
> ing any pious or spiritual work without regard to its suitability to
> the actual needs of our soul. There are many spiritual books
> which would be beneficial to some, but harmful to others. For ex-
> ample, books which excite the imagination and emotions, such as
> the biographies of extraordinary saints, would be harmful to peo-
> ple who are over-emotional or sentimental or who are endowed
> with an unusually vivid imagination. Likewise, literature dealing
> with death, judgment, and hell is very profitable to some but
> harmful to others.

Imitatio Christi et Mariae

Christian perfection is sometimes said to be an "ideal" or a "value"
which we seek to approximate, but can never reach. Christian spirituality, however, is not about "ideals" or "values," but about the living God
and his great historic acts. God's creation of us in grace was an historic
event; it really happened, even if we have no documents from eyewitnesses. The entrance of sin into the world which deprived humanity
of grace was a historic event, even if we know it happened only from
its consequences. And God's plan to heal the effects of sin, to save us,
to restore his creation, and to lead it to the perfect fulfillment he intended for it, is manifest in historic events, culminating finally in God's
full self-revelation in the incarnation of his Son, Jesus Christ, who is no
myth but a real human being, one of us, living and dying and rising at
the center of our human history. In Jesus, God's love is not an ideal
merely to be approximated but a reality perfectly fulfilled in a unique
human life.

In his *Summa Theologiae* Parts II and III, Aquinas moves from an
abstract analysis of what it is to be a good human being to its concrete,
real, historical fulfillment in Jesus Christ. Without that historical reality
all that had gone before would be mere fantasy, mere myth. In Jesus'
life, death, and rising, in his cross which binds his whole history

together, we are shown what it means to "be perfect," truly to love, truly to be a fully human and fully graced human person.

Hence, the Dominican tradition supports the view that true perfection is the *imitatio Christi*, discipleship, the following of Jesus, although Aquinas more often says it is the *imitatio Dei*, "to which is accomplished only through Christ and by the power of his Holy Spirit, that is, by grace. As St. Louis de Montfort says:[31]

> Can we love what we do not know? Can we love dearly what we know only a little? Why is it we love so little the Eternal and Incarnate Wisdom, the Lord Jesus, except because we do not know Him, or only a little? Few there are who, like the Apostle Paul, have studied as it is necessary that supreme science of Jesus, although it is the noblest, most delightful, most useful, and most necessary of all the sciences and arts of heaven and earth....What has an archer won if he hits the target but not the bulls-eye? What profit is to us all the other sciences necessary for salvation, if we do not know that of Jesus Christ who is "the one thing necessary," the center on which all this knowledge should converge?

The coming of the Holy Spirit sent by the Father as a result of Christ's obedience, is also a historic reality manifested in the origin, growth and life of the church and of true Christians. The Holy Spirit is the interior revelation of God, as the incarnation was its exterior, visible revelation, and completes it in us. The Holy Spirit is properly named "The Gift of God," i.e., uncreated grace, and thus the source of grace as it is a transformation of the creation.

Spiritual directors must, therefore help those they guide to accept no other model of Christian perfection than the God revealed in Jesus Christ, and must trust in no other power to transform them into the image of God than the power of Christ's Holy Spirit, the power of divine grace. Too often directors make clients into their disciples, rather than into disciples of Jesus Christ, and too often beginners try to imitate imperfect or even wrong models of sanctity which attract them or are mere fads. Too often, also, they place their trust in devotional attractions, pilgrimages, spiritual gimmicks and techniques, instead of in the grace of the Holy Spirit.

The Dominican tradition of spirituality has always been prudent and cautious in its teaching on the Blessed Virgin Mary, as witness St. Thomas' hesitation to accept her immaculate conception until it could be shown to be consistent with the more fundamental dogma that all human beings must be redeemed by Jesus Christ, and the long controversy in which Aquinas' followers opposed the definition of the dogma. None of this, however, was because they lacked devotion to her or wanted a "low mariology" rather than the "high mariology" enthusiastically promoted by the sons of St. Francis.

For Thomists, who of course now wholeheartedly accept the solemn definitions of the church concerning Mary, the fundamental truth about her in the plan of salvation is that she is the Mother of God because of her faithful obedience to God by her, "Let it be done to me according to your word." By this fiat, uttered not only in her own behalf but as the representative of all of faithful Israel, and indeed of all humanity, Mary reversed the disobedience of Eve. Since her Son is the new Adam, the Father of all the redeemed who form his mystical body, the Christian community, Mary is also the mother of the church. As the Holy Spirit overshadowed her in the conception of her Son, so through her prayers with the apostles and the holy women at Pentecost, the same Spirit has completed Christ's body. Indeed, as the chief member of the church under the headship of Christ, she is the church, the bride of the risen Christ, who has already been taken up with him in glory, body and soul in her assumption, so that we and the rest of the church may follow Jesus and Mary in the final resurrection in the kingdom of the Father.

But, "Why do we need Mary, when we have Christ?" is the obvious question. The Thomistic answer, given by so many Dominican preachers of the rosary, and in particular by St. Louis Grignion de Montfort, is that Christ as God is all-sufficient, but because he has chosen to save us by becoming one of us in the incarnation, Mary plays an essential role in our salvation, as his mother and as ours, just as does the church and its sacraments, all of which receive their efficacy entirely from Christ, true God and true man. Today Christian feminists are often troubled by the fact that the incarnation took place in a male rather than a female human nature, thus seeming to marginalize women. The only answer they have found to this is to treat the gender of the incarnate one as of no theological significance, but a mere concession by God to the patriarchalism of the world in which the incarnation took place.

From a Thomistic point of view any such answer minimizes the incarnational character of God's revelation and smacks of the Platonism that ignores the body and over-spiritualizes the Bible. It seems much more adequate to say that in giving to a woman an essential role in the incarnation, even if she is not herself the incarnate one, God has given a true equality between male and female in the plan of salvation. Man and woman play complementary roles which unite them in the equality of mutual love. As St. Paul said, "Woman is not independent of man or man of woman in the Lord. For just as woman came from man, so man is born of woman, but all things are from God" (1 Cor 11:11–12).

The noted French Dominican, A. D. Sertillanges says:[32]

> We have but one model: Jesus Christ. Nevertheless, in a certain sense, we have two, just as, looking on a calm sea, at nightfall, we have two fields of stars...Mary is to us, then, a faithful mirror, but a mirror conscious of its function, consenting to it, powerful for it, knowing and loving the light reflected and them who are illuminated thereby, with a capacity for communicating that light and opening the eyes of those upon whom it shines.

Thus the Christian journey is a following of Jesus, but for that very reason a following of Mary who walks at his side as his revered companion and wholly beloved. She thus becomes the standard of graced humanity for women as women, as Jesus is for men as men. Of course, this does not mean that men do not look to her too, since they see in her those aspects of Jesus' own personality which are more explicit in her as woman, and which enable them to recognize similar gifts in themselves. And the same for women with respect to Jesus.

Unfortunately, some Christian feminists even resent the idea that Mary can be their model of womanhood, since she lived a domestic life and not one of a public career which feminists justly claim should also be open to them. But they should remember that neither do many men find Jesus a model of manhood, since he was so unlike the kind of macho image they seek for themselves. The real problem is that our spiritual writers and artists have often given us an unbiblical picture of Mary as a pale, passive, sweetly vapid adolescent, not at all the valiant woman of the Bible. The spiritual fatherhood of Jesus and the virgin motherhood of Mary were far broader than any narrow domestic scene.

Theirs is a spiritual parentage of the whole world to come, of the kingdom of God. No career was grander than theirs, the liberation of all humanity from the powers of death and hell.

One of the special difficulties that Dominicans have always been concerned about is the union of the contemplative and the active life demanded by the ministry of the word. The thirteenth-century Dominican biblical scholar Hugh of St. Cher points out in a remarkable passage that in Mary these two types of life are reconciled:[33]

> The Blessed Virgin was both Martha and Mary—Martha because of her busyness in good deeds, Mary because of her quiet in holy contemplation. For she was a Martha to Elizabeth her pregnant kinswoman, caring for her three months. She was Martha when she gave all the attentive care that should be given to the poor to her own Son in his poverty. For she received him in her womb, like a guest in the house. Naked, she clothed him in human flesh and wrapped him in swaddling clothes. When he was hungry and thirsty she gave him her milk to drink and fondled him. When he was a weak infant she not only visited him, as we are commanded (Mt 25:31–46), but dwelled with him, played with him. When he was imprisoned and crucified, she came to him, so that the words, "Martha was busy with all the details of hospitality" (Lk 10:40) truly apply to her. At the same time the Blessed Virgin was Mary in listening to the Lord, pondering in her heart what she had heard and seen of those things foretold by the prophets. Whence it follows, "Mary seated herself at the Lord's feet and listened to his words" (Lk 10:39), and it is also written "Mary kept all these words" (Lk 2:51) in the secret of her heart and afterwards told them to the writers of the Gospels. For she taught Matthew, who first wrote much of her, while in Luke's Gospel which speaks of these two sisters, the Blessed Virgin is many times commended.

Consequently spiritual directors should help the men and women they direct to a profound understanding of what true womanhood is as manifest in Mary and true manhood as manifest in her Son, who resembles her to a degree that no other son has ever resembled his mother. Only in this way can the special gifts God has given us as men and women come to full Christian realization.

Chapter 4

======

The Ministry of Spiritual Direction

The Need for Spiritual Direction

It is not obvious why a Christian who is guided by the Bible and the interior light of the Holy Spirit needs spiritual direction. Yet even Protestants have considered that one of the roles of a good pastor is the individual spiritual counseling of his people who come to him, although the notion of "spiritual direction" as Catholics have practiced it is not so common among them. Yet any responsible spiritual director must ask that question, *Is the ministry I am undertaking really needed?* and must find an honest and adequate answer before undertaking such a task.

It is to be feared that for some directors the real answer to that query is that it is the director who needs that ministry rather than his or her clients. I will discuss that point later. Here we are asking whether and why Christians need to be directed? Certainly the Catholic answer is that every Christian needs to be guided by God on his journey to God, since the risks of getting side-tracked or turning back are great. God has given us that direction gradually through his prophets and scribes of the Old Testament, and finally and clearly in the teaching and life of Jesus, then through his Holy Spirit in the church and its tradition and the New Testament, and that tradition continues today in our bishops and pastors who have been ordained as our shepherds.

The fourteenth-century Dominican spiritual director of a group of "Friends of God," Venturino de Bergamo, stated the traditional answer as follows:[34]

If you have any of the aforesaid temptations, do not long conceal them, but reveal them to a wise and discrete confessor and to other special persons so that they can consider what counsel, help,

75

or comfort they can give you from their own experience of temptation or their light of wisdom and holiness. For that remedy the saints have much commended since it said in the *Lives of the Fathers* that certain monks who were advanced in the life of holiness but who contemned and despised the counsel and help of the holy fathers concerning their temptations came to a bad end. And it happens to many others that by the will of God they escape their temptations because of the humility they show in seeking the counsel and help of the holy fathers in their temptations.

Yet in spite of all these ways in the church that God guides us very surely on our path, today we often feel in the dark. For many the guidance of the scriptures seems to have been obscured by modern science and made much more complicated by critical biblical scholarship and the comparative study of religions. The guidance of the inner light of the Holy Spirit seems obscured by the extravagant claims of some charismatics and by the suspicions of modern psychology. The guidance of the pope and bishops has been undermined by their apparent conservatism and the criticisms of theologians and the press. As for one's local clergy they are mistrusted, not so much because of scandalous incidents, as because they seem insensitive to many very real problems, and lacking in anything more than moralistic insights, men of superficial piety rather than deep spirituality. Even religious priests, once revered as of deeper spirituality than the diocesan clergy, seem to be members of communities whose troubles and desertions seem to indicate spiritual confusion rather than wisdom. Finally, the current trend for religious sisters and for laypeople, sometimes with rather superficial theological training, to become self-appointed spiritual directors without any special evaluation or certification by the church, seems to have produced highly eclectic forms of direction which depend more on oriental religions and Jungian psychology than on tested Christian experience.

The Dominican tradition generally never institutionalized the office of "spiritual director" in the way that the Jesuits developed this office, with its whole process of spiritual exercises and personal direction. The development of that art seems to have been a special contribution to the church by the Society of Jesus, and it was built into the seminary system for the training of the diocesan seminarians, where the spiritual director of the seminary is an office comparable only to that of the rector, not only in the guidance of the seminarians, but in their approval for ordination. Yet neither did the Dominican tradition reject the practices introduced by the Jesuits, as is evident in the work of Antonine Chesnois, O.P., (d. 1685), *The Idea of Christianity or the Conduct of Sanctifying Grace* (Rouen, 1672) in which he insists that spiritual direction is necessary, that it take place in a sacred setting, should not be prolonged by idle talk, once a week, or once a month by correspondence.

The Dominican tradition never saw the prior of the local houses as the spiritual father in the manner of the abbot in the monastic tradition. It is true that priors had a responsibility of guidance, and of giving occasional spiritual conferences to the friars, but in recent times they were forbidden to hear the confessions of their subjects (except in an emergency) and their direction was general rather than individualized, confined largely to matters of observance of the Rule and Constitutions.

The prior, however, does not act alone, but in consultation with the house chapter which, at least in smaller houses, would include all the solemnly professed members. Thus the fraternal correction and guidance of individual friars ultimately is an expression of the insights of all the friars experienced in religious life and committed to it. All have a responsibility to help each individual member advance spiritually.

The Dominican assumption seems to have been that the friar was guided in his spiritual growth primarily by simply living in a Dominican community and sharing its life. If in attempting to do so he met special problems which involved problems of conscience, these could be discussed with the approved confessors, or if they concerned his relations with the community or his vocation or ministry they could be discussed with the superiors concerned, prior or provincial, or other officials, or with more experienced brothers that he might want to consult. For the novices and the students their respective Masters were available for such consultation, but ordinarily not for confessional matters.

At the time of the annual retreat, which was generally only a week long, the retreat master, who was generally selected for his reputation as someone of spiritual experience and wisdom, could be consulted. In some provinces or priories, perhaps under Jesuit influences, spiritual directors were appointed among whom the novices and students might choose, but this was not expected of the priests, although some, in fact, continued to have spiritual directors of their own choosing.

Dominican nuns generally sought such spiritual direction as they received from the chaplain or the regular confessor who made periodic visits to the convent, as did the sisters who were freer to go out of the convent for confession or counseling. Canon law permitted both nuns and sisters to send for a confessor if they wished, but this was often not very practical. Dominican women, like the men, often waited for the annual retreat to speak of special difficulties to the retreat master.

In fact, it is by no means obvious that it is necessary or even possible for every sincere Christian to have a "regular" spiritual director. To some it seems a kind of spiritual luxury which tends to promote an excessive self-centeredness, a kind of spiritual narcissism, not unlike the obsession for psychoanalysis.

Dominican spirituality, as I have indicated, puts the accent on objective, public truth, rather than on preoccupation with subjective life. We come to know ourselves, not so much by looking inward, as looking outward on our relations to the world and to people.

But when this has all been said, we have the words of the most profound students of the Dominican tradition, Ven. Juan Arintero and Reginald Garrigou-Lagrange, that spiritual direction is a very real need for the Christian. Thus Arintero writes (*The Mystical Evolution*, vol. 1, p.308):

> …To overthrow self-love, to deny our own will, and to avoid the snares of self-complacency, it is necessary that we have a good spiritual director to whom we subject ourselves with docility in all things so that he may teach us how to exercise ourselves in prayer and the good practice of all the virtues. Although virtue should observe the just mean of prudence, no one is a worthy judge of his own case. A good director will help us to overcome our difficulties and to conquer obstacles, and will preserve us from the wiles of our enemies.

St. Vincent Ferrer, O.P., in his *Treatise on the Spiritual Life*, had long ago given the same advice:[35]

> Therefore it must be understood that one more easily and in shorter time is able to attain perfection, if he has an instructor by whose guidance he may be led, whose obedience in all acts small and great he may totally follow, that if he attempts to perfect him-

self, no matter how brilliant his intellect may be, and even if he has books in which he can see the whole structure of the virtues displayed. I would even go so far as to say that Christ will never minister his grace, without which we can do nothing, if a man has someone by whom he can be instructed and led, yet neglects, or takes no care to take advantage of the direction of this other, believing himself to be self-sufficient, and able of himself to investigate and discover what is useful for his salvation. For that way of obedience is the royal way which leads men, to whom the Lord lends his support, sure footedly to the top of the ladder of perfection. All the holy Desert Fathers kept to this path and, in short, all who have attained to perfection have taken it. Unless perhaps God has himself instructed, by the privilege of a singular grace, those who lacked anyone else to instruct them externally; since then the Divine Pity itself supplied what was not found exteriorly, if nevertheless these approach God with humble and fervent hearts.

And the great Thomistic commentator Jean Poinsot (John of St. Thomas) explained this in terms of the Gift of the Holy Spirit of Counsel:[36]

The gift of counsel does have a certitude from the Holy Spirit, not indeed that of faith, but a prudential certitude founded upon the motion of the Holy Spirit. It is of the essence of this prudential certitude that, when the things themselves are in doubt or are obscure, there should be a test and an examination by others who have the gift in more excellent manner and who penetrate and understand better the standards of faith by which these spiritual sways and motions are to be examined. Since in doubt of this kind the Holy Spirit does not ordinarily give counsel and interior certitude without a dependence upon the examination of others, the gift of counsel moves us to this examination. The Holy Spirit wishes to prove that the spirit is from God. He also wishes to have us proceed humbly without presuming that of ourselves we can order all things which belong to the gift of counsel. The counsel of God is especially a counsel of humility and examination. Hence a person should not be led by a private spirit, but by one which has been examined.

Just as today as we believe that everyone should have a physician and at least regular physical examinations, and as we increasingly believe that psychological counseling is required even by normal people at least in certain difficult periods of life, so it would seem that every Christian would profit from occasional sessions with a spiritual counselor, and that it is best that this counselor be someone who knows the client well, i.e., a regular spiritual director. Of course, in our actual situation, most Catholics cannot in fact easily find such a competent director, even as today many persons in our society do not have access to a physician, and fewer still to a psychotherapist.

It would seem that in ideal circumstances the church and a Christian society would be so organized that spiritual guidance at all levels, from the most general pastoral care to individualized spiritual direction would be available to all, and especially that within each local church, and above all within each religious community this would be a normal feature of life. In such a situation most Christians would not need frequent individual direction, but it would be available to them when needed. Frequent consultation would be necessary only at crisis points in spiritual growth, and regular direction would be adequately provided by the daily regimen. Plato once said that a society with many physicians is a sick society, and so in an ideal Christian society we should expect that there would not be extensive recourse to specialists in spiritual direction.

In our actual world the church is so beset by non-Christian influences that this ideal environment is not to be expected. Individuals have to make the best of their situation, confident in the providence of God who never fails us if we seek him sincerely and who knows how to provide us with the direction we need even when the regular means of obtaining it seem absent. St. Vincent Ferrer goes on, after the passage quoted above to say:

And indeed today, alas for us miserable ones, it seems that no one can be found who will instruct others concerning the life of perfection! Rather if a man wishes to seek God, he finds many who hinder him and almost no one to help him. Therefore it is necessary that a man run to God with all his heart and beg to be instructed by him with unceasing prayer and humility of heart, and to throw himself on God, totally committing himself to him, that he might be received kindly as an orphan without a father, a father who wants no one to perish, but wishes that all should come to the knowledge of the truth (1 Tm 4). Therefore I direct my words to you who with a great longing of the heart desire to come to God, who long to attain perfection that they may be useful to the souls of others. To you now I direct my words, who with simple, not double hearts, approach God; who seek to penetrate the innermost depths of virtue, who by the path of humility desire to attain the glory of God's majesty. What we can conclude, however, is that every Christian who wants to make consistent progress in the spiritual life should make a serious effort to get good spiritual direction, and not simply rely on their own judgment alone.

And Melchior Cano, speaking of the person who seems to be suffering from spiritual "burn-out" says:[37]

Another excellent remedy is to subject your will to the will of others who know how to direct you, since no one who has not learned to subordinate his will to the will of another will ever emerge victorious. Indeed I realize that in our days there are few directors who can straighten our path by their teaching, spurring on the weak by their example, arousing the indifferent by their exhortations, quickening the negligent and the spiritually dead by their own dedicated lives. However, there is no dearth of books available to help you grow in fervor.

We should conclude, therefore, that those seeking to advance spiritually should seek to find a good guide, a regular confessor or spiritual counselor who is competent and consult them as frequently as, in the judgment of the counselor, this is genuinely useful. If they cannot find such a director, they should at least go to confession regularly, make regular retreats, and with the approval of one of these advisors, set up a plan of life (a *regula vitae*) and of spiritual reading which will provide them with an objective standard of guidance. This individual guidance should be consistent with the milieu in which they live.

A person living in a highly regulated religious community or in a well-functioning parish should for the most part be content with the guidance this provides, unless special difficulties arise. But those living in a milieu which is unchristian or simply confused, need to provide for themselves special means to receive the guidance they require. The growth of support-groups of various kinds is an indication that this is a felt need of many today.

The Goals of Spiritual Direction

Spiritual directors must ask themselves honestly: *What am I trying to do for those I direct?* St. Catherine of Siena, troubled by the fact that in counseling people she often seemed to be able to read their minds even before they spoke, said to God,[38]

> Sometimes people will come to me or to another of your servants asking for counsel in their desire to serve you and wanting me to instruct them. I know gentle, eternal God, that you have already told me, "I am one who takes delight in few words and many deeds." Still, if it would please your kindness to say a few more words on this, you would be doing me a great favor.

God the Father, in answer to her question, gave her three rules to follow so as to avoid depending merely on her intuitions, which he said were not always to be trusted:

> (1) Even if your neighbors' sins are clearly shown to your spirit not just once or twice but many times, you should still not confront them with specific sins. Rather when they come to visit you, you should correct their bad habits in a general way and lovingly and kindly plant the virtues in their place, adding severity when you must....So let silence or a holy argument for virtue be in your mouth (c. 102).

> (2) I will then, and so should you—you and my other servants—that you concentrate on coming to know yourselves perfectly, so that you may more perfectly know my goodness to you. Leave this and every other kind of judgment, which belongs to me, and take up compassion with hunger for my honor and the salvation of souls. And with restless longing preach virtue and reprove vice in yourself and in others in the manner I have just described to you (c. 103).

> 3) Reprove yourself if ever the devil or your own short-sighted-ness should do you the disservice of making you want to force all

my servants to walk in the same path you yourself follow, for this would be contrary to the teaching given you by my Truth (c. 104).

To these principles God then added the test she is to use in determining whether the religious experiences of persons are authentic or not:

> The sign is the gladness and hunger for virtue that remain in the soul after the visitation, especially if she is anointed with the virtue of true humility, and set ablaze with divine charity (c. 106).

And the Father explains that while "gladness" is an effect of a true religious experience, it can be illusory unless it is conjoined with a real "hunger for virtue" and especially "humility" and "charity." These rules, which are classical and rooted in teachings of the desert fathers, amount to this:

> (1) Directors must begin with an attitude of acceptance of the person, not prejudgment.
>
> (2) Directors must recognize their own limitations and patiently await to see what the Holy Spirit is doing in the client.
>
> (3) Directors must not mold their clients after themselves but after Christ.

Another way to describe the director's work is to say it consists first in instructing the client in the principles of the Christian life, second in encouraging their efforts and successes, third in confronting them when necessary with hard truths about themselves that they are trying to deny (note in the first quotation above that God says to Catherine "adding severity when you must"). Catherine's letters are filled with encouragement to those to whom she writes, and she knows how to confront when necessary.

The role of instruction, however, is a specifically Dominican note. Some writers on our topic, following the lead of psychotherapists who denounce "preaching" to clients and advocate a "non-directive approach," seem to discourage theological instruction during spiritual direction and advocate simply helping the client analyze their own religious experience. The Dominican tradition, however, constant in its faith in the efficacy of preaching and the importance of intelligent understanding of matters of faith, emphasizes good instruction.

The first 87 chapters of Catherine of Siena's *Dialogue* are actually a thorough catechesis on the basic truths of the Catholic faith and the Christian's moral obligations. After all, the goal of direction is union with God in the Holy Spirit through the incarnate Word, and unless the Christian keeps this goal clearly in mind and has an increasingly true understanding of what that goal is and means, there can be no motive for progress. One must be drawn to God in love by seeing more and more how lovable God is.

Of course it is true that a director makes a very serious mistake if he or she uses up the time of counseling with wordy sermons or moralizing exhortations. That is "preaching," but it is bad preaching. The Dominican ideal is "doctrinal preaching," a ministry of the word which enlightens the mind in such a way as to enkindle the heart. The good director will listen much, and say little, but she will not fail, in what little she says, to instruct, to deepen the client's theological understanding, relating the client's experiences to the great truths of the Creed.

The Qualities of a Good Director

Before they direct others, those engaged in this ministry must ask themselves, *Am I qualified to direct others, when I need to be guided myself?*

As we have just seen, God told St. Catherine that if she was to counsel others she must grow in self-knowledge. Psychoanalytic practice has insisted that before becoming an analyst the physician must be him or herself analyzed. Those engaged in counseling others need to be counseled themselves. As surgeons know they must disinfect their hands before they touch patients, lest they infect them further, so spiritual directors must be spiritually purified lest they infect their clients with new sinfulness. The tendency of some directors to use clients to assert their own power is demonic, and there are many historic examples of the ruin it has caused.

Directors can also misuse their clients by becoming dependent on them for flattery and for affection, as psychotherapists sometimes do; and of course this sometimes ends in illicit sexual relationships or at least unhealthy co-dependencies.

The Ven. Juan Arintero in a passage on the qualifications of a direc-tor [39] quotes St. Teresa of Avila as saying that "it is better for the soul to be without a director than to be badly directed" (p. 311). Summarizing the teaching of St. John of the Cross, Arintero says that a director should be "at once wise, zealous, discreet and experienced, or at least well-versed in the ways of the Lord" (p. 309). The defect of learned academics who are not themselves persons of prayer and zeal is that they will be insensitive to the work of the Spirit. The defect of pious but unlearned directors is that they tend to insist that a client follow the same path that they have followed when this may not be the one the Lord has chosen for their clients, the very danger that God warned St. Catherine against.[40]

Since the church has approved the writings of Catherine, Teresa and other great spiritual writers, and since there are reliable theological studies of classical spirituality such as those of Garrigou-Lagrange and Arintero, it should be obvious that no director should presume to engage in this ministry without solid acquaintance with the classical tradition. To believe that one can be a good director, when one is only acquainted with some current popular books, or with a spiritual tech-nique that is often very different from the Christian tradition is irre-sponsible. Arintero points out that it is essential that spiritual directors have sufficient learning and experience. "Otherwise, like one blind man leading another, they both fall into the ditch. Inexperienced and ignorant directors do more damage than good to souls" (p. 309).

Above all, spiritual directors must be motivated by a truly Christian love for those they are trying to help. They need to heed the advice of St. Vincent Ferrer, O.P., to confessors: [41]

When hearing confession, you should always radiate the warmest charity. Whether you are gently encouraging the fainthearted or putting the fear of God into the hardhearted, the penitent should feel that you are motivated only by pure love. Therefore, speak in a pleasant, friendly way before you use words that will prod his conscience. Finally, if you truly want to help the soul of your neighbor, you should approach God first with all your heart. Ask him simply to fill you with charity, the greatest of all virtues; with it you can accomplish what you desire.

The Chapter of Faults and Support Groups

In the direction of those who live in a Christian community, religious or lay, an important question for directors to ask themselves is: *How does my guidance take into account that which my client is already receiving from his or her community? Am I contradicting that guidance or supporting it?* A fundamental rule for anyone seeking spiritual guidance is not to subject themselves to more than one director, or to run from one to another, since this can only result in confusion, discouragement, and lack of progress. Therefore, the spiritual director of an individual must seek always to work within community guidance, unless it becomes clear that such guidance is seriously harmful. In the latter case, the director must address the problem very frankly but with great prudence, in order to help the client decide how the problem is to be handled, if necessary by leaving the community, but much more commonly by finding ways to be faithful to his or her original commitment in a milieu whose harmful tendencies and influences have to be courageously and patiently resisted. It is not at all certain, however, that in any but extreme cases, a religious is likely to find a new community that will be better than the old.

A feature of the Dominican tradition, which today is often neglected but which is of considerable significance, is the retention in the *Primitive Constitutions* (which were adopted under Dominic's own leadership) of the traditional monastic "Chapter of Faults." This was a periodic meeting of a local community, its prior presiding, at which the friars individually and publicly confessed their personal infractions of the rule and constitutions and "proclaimed" to the others the infractions by other brethren which they had observed, and then asked the forgiveness of the community or of particular individuals they had offended. They each then prostrated themselves (made the *venia*) and while prostrate received the correction of the prior and a penance to perform. The prior might then make a general admonition to the community or speak words of commendation, thanks, and encouragement, and finally gave an "absolution from faults," freeing the individuals and community from further penalties than those already imposed.

In some houses the novices, clerical students, and cooperator brothers might have their chapter apart from that of the priests, with their own immediate superior presiding. Provincial and general chapters began with similar proceedings, and provincials and Masters of the Order were themselves required to confess their faults against the rule.

St. Dominic had emphatically insisted that the rule and constitutions of his order should bind, not under sin, but only under penalty, since he had no desire to increase the friars' burden of sin but only to provide them with a means to virtue. Consequently, the "faults" confessed or proclaimed in chapter were not sins (those were to be confessed in the sacrament of penance), but infractions of the rule and constitutions, and had its biblical warrant in Jesus' teaching on "fraternal correction" (Mt 18:15–20) and its patristic warrant especially in the Rule of St. Augustine.

This is not the place to discuss how this ancient exercise might be revised to serve more effectively the present needs for direction than the often merely formal and routine way in which in the pre-Vatican II period the Chapter of Faults was conducted. In the United States Dominican provinces, while the Chapter of Faults was regularly held, at least in houses of formation, and the confession of faults made, the "proclamation" of the faults of others was omitted as contrary to the America ethos. Since Vatican II, however, the chapter in U.S. Dominican communities has tended to take the form of open discussions where feedback is given on such topics as "How does *your* behavior cause *me* problems," and the discussion seldom turns on the Rule or the Constitutions as such.

It is important, however, to see what the Chapter of Faults was supposed to contribute to Dominican spiritual direction. Clearly it was based on the belief, expressed by one of the popes, "Show me the friar who keeps his rule, and I will canonize him." Two qualifications have to be made to this saying. First, St. Paul, whose epistles novices were recommended by the old constitutions to memorize, teaches us that we are not saved by the observance of laws, but by faith, i.e., one can, like the Pharisees, strain at the gnats of monastic observance, while swallowing the camel of offenses against charity. An observance of the rules that is not motivated by love of God and neighbor cannot sanctify. That is stated plainly enough by the Rule of St. Augustine which begins:

Before all things, my most dear brothers, we must love God and after Him our neighbor for these are the principal commands which have been given us. The following things, then, we direct you, who live in the monastery, to observe. First, that you should dwell together in unity in the house and be of one mind and one heart in God, remembering that this is the end for which we are collected here.

The second qualification was made by the Lord himself (Mt 19:16–30 and parallels) when, after telling the rich young man that to gain eternal life he must keep the commandments and commending him when he claimed to have done so, Jesus said, "Sell all you have, give to the poor, and come follow me!" In other words, Christian sanctity goes beyond any rules.

Yet there is a truth in the pope's saying that the road to sanctity is obedience to the rules and constitutions. For these, like the ten commandments, of which they are really only a concrete expression, provide us with a spiritual direction regarding the fundamental elements of a Christian and consecrated life. If we carry them out faithfully from true Christian motives and interpret them in the light of these goals, they keep us on the right path to holiness. Jesus and his faithful disciple, St. Paul, did not repudiate the laws of the Old Testament, they observed them carefully and approved their sincere observance by others.

The Rule of St. Augustine is deeply infused with the spirit of the primitive Christian community in Jerusalem as described in Acts (4:32–35) and the Constitutions, reduced to their essentials by the revision of the General Chapter of 1968 after Vatican II, provide a way of life in which the members of a community guide each other by their mutual insights, under the headship of a "first brother" (prior) whom they have elected, after prayerful mutual discernment, to act as their pastor in the living of their lives. This will be effective, however, only if the Chapter of Faults in some form makes possible a regular evaluation of the success and failures of the friars and of the community as a whole in living up to the goal to which they are covenanted.

It may also be suggested that, even in family life, something like a chapter of faults might be incorporated into family prayers such as a few moments in which the members of the family might ask mutual pardon for open faults against the peace and good order of domestic life. Also, today the growth of group dynamics and support groups, although their purpose is generally more psychological than moral or spiritual, is serving for many people the objective recognition and catharsis of failings that somewhat resembles the function of an effective chapter of faults. This can be incorporated into group direction. It must be remembered, however, that this is proper for external faults that have a public character, but that private, internal faults and sins belong more appropriately to the confessional.

The Three Processes of Spiritual Growth

Spiritual directors guide others in spiritual growth. Hence they must ask themselves, as a parent asks about a growing child, "What are the processes by which spiritual growth normally takes place and in what sequence?" Obviously, any journey has a beginning, a middle, and an end, and St. Thomas Aquinas speaks of beginners, proficients, and the perfect on the path of Christian perfection. He also uses the terminology of the Pseudo-Dionysius that seems to have originated with Origen and was used by St. Gregory of Nyssa and other Eastern fathers which divides the spiritual journey into the "three ages" or the "three ways": the purgative, the illuminative and the unitive.

St. Catherine of Siena speaks of "three stairs" of the Bridge (Christ) which are the three powers of the soul, and connects these with the "three stages" of the "imperfect, the more perfect, and the most perfect," of which she says, "The first is a mercenary, the second my faithful servant, the third my child who loves me with no regard for selfish interests."[42] Finally, she speaks of them as dwelling at the feet, the heart, and the head of Christ crucified.

Dominican writers after St. John of the Cross have generally accepted his view that these three phases of spiritual growth are normally separated from each other by spiritual "nights," the "dark night of the soul" marking the transition from the purgative to the illuminative phase, and the "dark night of the spirit" from the illuminative to the unitive phase.

In the following chapters we will discuss what is proper to these three phases, but it is essential to realize: (a) that this paradigm is an abstraction which is realized in very different ways in concrete cases, and may not be clearly apparent in the life of any given Christian; (b) the underlying reason for these three phases of the spiritual journey is that they each reflect the predominance of one of three fundamental processes that go on simultaneously throughout the journey, namely, the process of spiritual purgation, illumination, and union.

For example, every time a Christian worthily participates in the celebration of the eucharist, there is : (1) a process of repentance and conversion from sin, i.e., purgation, formulated as the act of contrition at the beginning of mass; (2) a process of illumination in listening to the scripture readings and the sermon and in the recitation of the Creed; (3) a process of union in joining with Christ in the eucharistic prayer and receiving him in holy communion.

For beginners on the spiritual journey, the process of conversion from sin tends to be the predominant task. For the more mature in the spiritual life, the process of positive growth in character through authentic virtue takes over. Finally, the Christian of stable and well-balanced virtue is prepared to enter into that intimate and constant union with Christ that anticipates the union of heaven. In each individual, however, depending on their fidelity to their loving search for God, but also on God's particular providence for each, the interweaving of these processes will take different forms.

Therefore, in the three concluding chapters of this book, I will discuss each of these fundamental processes, as well as saying something of the stages in which they play the major role.

=====

Chapter 5

The Process of Purification

Original Blessing and Original Sin

Particularly in counseling beginners on the spiritual journey, the first issue that confronts the director concerns the true conversion and commitment of clients: *Have they sincerely renounced mortal sin and turned to God as the goal of their life?* Jesus' own preaching began with, "This is the time of fulfillment. The kingdom of God is at hand. Repent and believe in the gospel" (Mk 1:15). Repentance and conversion is the first step in the process of purification. What then is "sin" from which the Christian must be purified?

A story is told of St. Thomas Aquinas dining at the court of Louis IX, King of France. Thomas became so absorbed in thought that he forgot his food and suddenly startled the court by striking the table and exclaiming, "That settles the Manichees!" Whereupon the wise and saintly king sent for a secretary to write down Thomas' inspiration lest it be lost.[43] The Dominican Order was born from Dominic's horror at finding what inroads the Manichean (Albigensian) heresy had made among the Christians of southern France, a heresy that taught that the material creation is the work of an Evil God. No wonder, then, that the teaching of Genesis 1, that creation is not only good, but "very good," has always been a major theme of the Dominican tradition.

Recently this theme has been popularized by Matthew Fox in his many books on what he calls "creation-centered theology." These are so one-sided as to be, in my opinion, very unreliable guides to the Dominican tradition, but in his book *Original Blessing*[44] Fox has made the important point that we cannot understand "original sin" unless we place it in the context of the "original blessing," i.e., of the fact that humanity was created in God's image as wholly good, and indeed in God's grace as "very good." Yet as Fox himself admits, the world in

91

which we actually find ourselves is far from good. We live in a world of violence, injustice, racism, sexism, poverty, ignorance, lying propaganda, madness, disease, ecological devastation. And (which Fox tends to ignore) these social evils are rooted within each one of us in our own sensual bodies, hardened hearts, and deluded minds. It is this tragic paradox of a beautiful creation, of the garden of Eden become the ruined city of Zion, not one stone left on a stone, that is the meaning of the doctrine of original sin in which the spiritual journey begins.

In its modernized form, the Thomistic understanding of original sin (there are other theories) is that since the whole human race received its human nature from two original parents (or perhaps a group of parents whose offspring intermarried so that we can truly say that we form a single human community by descent) God intended us also to receive a graced nature through them. Just as Christian children now do receive the life of grace through their parents who profess the faith in their name and have them baptized, so if there had been no sin all human beings would have received the life of grace, not through a sacramental rite but through the very process of their conception by holy parents.

When the original parents by deliberate sin lost their state of grace for themselves they became incapable of transmitting it to their offspring, so that all historical humanity is conceived with a human nature deprived of its transformation by grace. This does not mean that children are born "sinners" in a strict sense, but that they are born deprived, through no sin of their own, of the grace that God intended they should have. They are victims of the sin of the first parents; they do not deserve punishment, but they share in some of the penalties which their parents deserved, just as without any merit of their own they would have shared in the gifts of grace which their parents should have transmitted to them.

Thus, for Aquinas, the deprivation of the original blessing of grace is transmitted to the whole person, body and soul, of the offspring by the parents at conception, and is principally the responsibility of the father as the efficient cause of their generation, secondarily of the mother as supplying the material cause of the child. God, who creates the soul, creates it for a merely natural body in which it inevitably contracts original sin, but in doing so God also intends to supply a remedy for this sad state of affairs resulting from original sin through the sacrament of baptism. That still so few children receive this rebirth to grace is not God's fault but the responsibility of the church's lack of missionary zeal and of the forces which oppose the spread of the gospel.

The term "original," however, does not refer merely to a single event at the beginning of time, although this has had a universal effect on all subsequent humanity. More fundamentally, "original" has two other references.

First, it refers to the origin of each human being, and hence includes not only the effect of the first parents' sin but of all the subsequent sins of the whole human race which have distorted the cosmos. Each of us, according to our place in history comes into a world which God planned would lead us most effectively to divine union, but today it is a world of violence, tyranny, poverty, ecological devastation, a babel of false ideologies which tend to lead us away from our true happiness and make virtue difficult and truth obscure.

Second, "original" refers not only to human origins but to the cosmic event of the fall of some of the created superhuman intelligences, the angels, through their own sin, far greater than human sin precisely because of their superior intelligence. The angels were also created in grace, but not in the beatific vision, which like human beings they could attain only by cooperation with God's grace. There was an original moment in which the angels had the choice to recognize in faith their need for God, or to reject God by a claim of absolute autonomy, which the devils, of whom Satan is chief, chose to do. Having rejected God, they also refused the services proper to them of enlightening angels less than themselves, and of maintaining the order and evolution of the universe. Consequently, human beings have now not only to suffer from the effects of human sin, but also the effects of angelic sin.

The emphasis the Dominican tradition has given to the role of the angels in spiritual life (is not St. Thomas called the "Angelic Doctor" because of this preoccupation?) may today be embarrassing to some, so let me quote an eminent Vatican II theologian, Yves Congar,[45]

There is…[a] more general reason for our indifference to the angels: this is the individualism and the moralism of our piety. It is true, of course, that a guardian angel is personally given to each of us, but the very fact that we have guardian angels is the result of a social plan, of salvation thought of in terms of the Church, of a corporate body, a plan, and point of view which has largely been lost sight of in the individualistic and moralistic mentality that has developed since the sixteenth century....The angels are our brethren in the supernatural world, our elder brothers; they watch over us and help us. We ourselves cannot know all the beauty of soul in a state of grace and St. John tells us that we do not yet know all that it means to be a child of God (1 Jn 3:2). But the angels see the full stature of a Christian soul. They who serve God in his intrinsic reality and who worship him, also serve him in us and in us profoundly reverence him.

Aquinas balances his terrifying view of the cosmic disorder produced by what St. Paul calls "the principalities,...the powers,...the world rulers of this present darkness,...the evil spirits of heaven" (Eph 6:12), first by pointing out that God's providence continues to rule the universe supremely, so that God permits no evil to occur that in the end he will not use as the occasion of a greater good for all created persons who turn to him for help. Consequently, Aquinas points out that while the evil agents can effect natural events and the human body, their power is restrained by God through the good angels. Moreover, since God alone can directly effect any created intelligence or free will, the devils cannot directly cause us to sin. They can tempt us, but we need not yield.

From the moment of the fall, according to the scriptures, God mercifully set in motion his work of salvation of the cosmos and of humanity. True, the fate of the angels, good and bad, was forever determined, because the clarity of their intelligences left them no possibility of perceiving their choices in any other way than they did at the moment of their decision. But, on the contrary, human beings, because they are embodied intelligences lacking clear vision and subject to changes of perception, a change of fundamental option remains a possibility throughout earthly life, and God has in his mercy willed to use this possibility to provide for them the means of conversion.

Thus each human being has come into a world which no longer unambiguously directs them toward God, and are subject in their own person, body and soul, by the very fact of their physical and psychological membership in the human community, to an interior warfare that makes them easy prey to all the forces that can turn them away from God.

Actual and Habitual Sin

The forces of original sin are at work in the child before fully self-conscious life and freedom begin and are qualified by the family in which they are born. Modern psychology has shown us how profound this conditioning can be, because the human child is so plastic, so quick to learn. It is at this stage affected mainly by the emotional climate and relationships of the family, and hence by psychological and ethical defects of parents and siblings, and possibly by violent abuse. Thus when the child's brain and inner senses reach the point that it begins to be self-conscious and thus to have a certain area of freedom (although this area at first is probably small and discontinuous) the child becomes capable of truly human and therefore moral acts for good or for bad.

Some religious educators today deny or minimize the possibility of sin in small children and consequently have urged that they not be introduced to sacramental confession until after first communion. Thomistic anthropology does not support this view and has generally accepted the traditional practice of having children begin to go to confession at the age of 6 or 7. A child who is able to do something that is humanly good (i.e., knowingly and freely chosen as good) is also able to do something that is humanly bad, able to sin. While undoubtedly this differs with individual children, experience seems to show that at about 6 or 7 children commonly do make choices in this way. If they are not ready to do what is humanly good, they are not usually considered ready to make their first communion, and if they are ready to do that, they are ready for confession.

But is it possible that a small child of 6 or 7 could commit a mortal sin? To many today this seems simply incredible, probably because of the legalistic understanding many Catholics have of morality. Since they think of morality and sin simply in terms of breaking rules, they cannot see how a child who still has little appreciation for which rules are "mortal" and which "venial" could possibly be guilty of more than venial sin. But once it is understood that morality is founded on the choice of true happiness and the means to it, it becomes apparent that a child can understand that its true happiness requires it to place love of its parents and siblings over mere selfishness. Surprising as it is, Thomistic analysis leads to the conclusion that the child's first truly human act necessarily involves a fundamental option. In this act a child begins to seek the happiness for which it was created, and in doing so it either commits itself to what its intelligence at that moment perceives as true happiness, or in the search for immediate satisfaction it rejects that standard and commits itself to an unreasonable goal of selfishness, a goal that it perceives is wrong and illusory.

Thus in its first step in moral life a child must head in the right direction toward God implicit in what it perceives as true happiness, or in the wrong direction in what it perceives as mere, momentary, pleasure. This choice, according to Thomist theory, is implicitly a choice of God or of self, and in the latter case is a mortal sin. Only after such a choice of an ultimate goal is possible, do venial sins become possible. Hence it is truly possible for a child at a very early age to begin a life of mortal sin and this is why also infant baptism is important because it provides graces that incline the child to make the right first choice, and why early confession makes sense.

The interviews of Robert Cole with children about their perceptions of their world and their moral responsibilities show us that we must have the utmost respect for the spiritual life of children.[46] A spiritual director who deals with children or with persons concerned about their relations to children, needs to become aware of what Jesus meant by saying, "Let the children come to me, and do not prevent them, for the kingdom of God belongs to such as these" (Mk 10:13). The child who starts on the right path to God and retains that childlike relation throughout life has very secure spiritual foundations. Unfortunately, it is at this level that many children lose their innocence and start on the wrong path. Closed off within themselves by self-centeredness and lack of trust of anything beyond themselves, only God's grace ministered through an understanding human love can ever free them.

In the adolescent there is an awakening from the rather narrow world of the child to all the possibilities of life. On the positive side, of course, this is an opening to the development of mature virtues, but on the negative side it means the awakening of all the powerful tendencies of fallen human nature, to autonomy and pride, to violence and domination, to greed and possessiveness, and to unbridled lust. Teenagers experience deep spiritual longings, the beginning of their vocation to family life, or to consecrated service to God, but are surrounded by powerful examples of greed, domination, and the pursuit of pleasure. Often their idealism is disillusioned by the defects they discover in their parents and other role models. If only they could find spiritual guides they could trust, who knew how to help them sort out these conflicting possibilities!

One often sees with sorrow how the young boy and girl whose personalities were so clean and open before adolescence become coarsened and even brutalized by adolescent rebellion and sexual dissipation. Perhaps the greatest danger of this perilous passage to adulthood is moral despair. The young man becomes so immersed in masturbation, then in going to prostitutes, or indulging in other forms of casual sex, and often in alcohol or drugs, so separated from his parents, so involved in dubious ways of making money, and in reckless behavior—things which his childhood training and now his own maturing common sense, tell him are foolish, weak, and simply bad, that he loses confidence in his own moral dignity and worth as a human being. The young girl becomes so immersed in seeking popularity with boys and competing with girls or in proving her independence and brains, that she engages in promiscuous sex, perhaps has abortions, engages in vicious gossip and rivalries, grasps for money, even sells herself, that she loses a sense of her own moral worth. Consequently, nothing is more important in the spiritual direction of adolescents than for the director to revive in them the conviction that they are not ruined goods, but that with the grace of God they can regain control of their lives and reconcile them with their consciences.

With adults the same problem of regaining the right path exists, but with those who have been truly converted the question becomes how to maintain a life without mortal sin. The spiritual director confronts what can be called the "morality gap" between what is objectively and subjectively right and wrong, a problem that belongs at the ethical level of the person, rather than the spiritual.

In an ideal condition of the church, the members of the church would have confidence that the magisterium, although not infallible in its ordinary moral teaching, is still the safest guide to what is objectively right and wrong, and would seek to obey this guidance without question, while accepting the responsibility to apply this teaching to individual situations. On the other hand, ideally the magisterium would trust the members of the church, once well instructed on the basic moral principles of the Catholic tradition to solve particular situations on the basis of their own experience and study.

Unfortunately, historically this ideal situation never prevails, notably in this period of transition in the church after Vatican II and in post-modern society. First, therefore, the spiritual director has to help the client come to the realization of how dangerous it is to trust judgments of moral objectivity simply on their social milieu or their own personal opinions, to see that they truly need the guidance of the Holy Spirit and that this guidance is given first of all through the church. At the same time, directors need to correct any tendencies in those they guide to adopt a merely mechanical obedience to the "rules" and instead to foster in them a willingness to assume personal responsibility in moral judgment without blaming problems on the church, the clergy, the director, or society.

Second, the director has to help the beginner come to an in-depth understanding of what the moral teaching of the church means and how to deal with situations where there are legitimate differences of opinion in the church. In this way the gap between objective morality and the subjective conscience of the client will be gradually lessened.

The first effect of sin is not the harm it does to others, which may or may not follow, but the intrinsic harm an immoral act does to the one who performs it. Since acts are immoral because contradictory to what our reason and faith tell us about our own human nature and its graced transformation, they wound us, they distort the image of God within us, they undermine the integrity of our character, they form bad habits (vices) within us, and they open us to temptation to further sins. They are gradual spiritual suicide. St. Paul tells us that sin makes us "slaves" because our freedom is given to us to reach true happiness, and the better we use it the freer we become; while when we misuse that freedom we sink deeper and deeper into a condition where we are more and more trapped and unable to seek true happiness. Christian courage is necessary to rise above these interior conflicts and to regain our freedom. As Vincent Contenson, O.P., in *Theology of the Mind and Heart*, said of our spiritual warfare:[47]

We have a General, who is often called in the Bible the Lord God of Hosts, so that he will conquer the foes that beset us. Therefore like good soldiers of Christ let us struggle, for no one will be crowned unless he conquers, nor will any conquer unless he fights, and no one can fight unless he has a foe whom he resists.

But if you are still afraid, be armed, be alert, watchful in peace, strong in battle, fearless in danger. But you may say when attacked from without and by enemies at home that the fight is too unfair for one man with but one heart to struggle with so great a crowd of enemies, for anger rushes in, avarice shouts, lust burns, ambition presses on; and there is no place free from snares, no age free of vices; therefore it is hard indeed not to be overcome by at least some of so many and such powerful and omnipresent foes constantly attacking us. In double array the old enemy lays siege, flattering us to deceive, terrifying us to break us down. So it is, I grant, and unless Christ came to our aid, the Christian could not conquer. Fly, therefore, to your General in battle, who conquers all the world with its terrors, errors, false loves!

Pathologies of Spiritual Life

The process of spiritual purification, therefore, is one of cutting the bonds that tie us to death. Because of the intimate relation between the different dimensions of the human personality, immorality, although at a different level of human personality than physical or mental health, tends to end in psychological and physical disease. The person who indulges immorally in pleasure may very well end an alcoholic, a drug addict, a victim of venereal disease, a suicide. But these levels of the personality should not be confused; a very wicked person may be psychologically and mentally normal; and a person of great virtue may suffer not only from physical disease, but also from mental disease. Hence the spiritual director must be sensitive to certain psychological problems closely associated with morality and with the purification from the effects of original and actual sin.

Even in the seventeenth century the problem of the discernment of authentic religious experience had occupied such theologians as Dominique Gravina, O.P. (d. 1643) who in his work, *Discerning True from False Visions and Revelations*, proposed four rules: true revelations must be (1) orthodox, (2) be clear and consistent (3), must stand the test of the tradition of spiritual discernment such as taught by Jean Gerson and Ignatius of Loyola; (4) must be analyzed by theologians; and Alphonse Costadau (d. 1725) who wrote a work in no less than twelve volumes, *A Historical and Critical Treatise on the Principal Signs of the Commerce of Spirits.*

But Dominican directors were also quite aware of psychological factors both in the diagnosis and therapy of human defects. For example, Melchior Cano, in his *Victory Over Self*, says this of what we today would call "depression,"[48]

> Industry and care, certainly, are necessary to cure this wound. In part we may disregard persons who are sad by reason of a melancholy temperament, since their cure is more with the province of the physician; and a prudent individual will not listen to a recital of spiritual illnesses until medical authority has first of all eliminated the possibility of physical or psychic ailments. If you are afflicted with sadness or depression, you should first of all determine whether this may be due to sin, because invariably the soul without God and virtue grows sad, especially when the transitory pleasures of the flesh fade, and the spirit feels the wounds left by sin. For this illness the sacrament of penance is the ideal medicine, since it removes the burden which weighs down the heart with sadness and remorse. If the illness arises from idleness, however, or is caused by some hidden suggestions of the enemy, the remedy is to occupy one's self with some appropriate activity; by this means, and especially prayer, health can readily be recovered. But if you are accustomed to grow sad because of opposition and frustration in your daily life, you should realize that the root of your trouble lies in favoring your own whims, desiring that everything should be done according to your own will. Consequently, a good remedy is continually to resolve to break with your own will and follow the wishes of another.

Today, we would also want to consult psychotherapists. Since there are two basic drives or groups of emotions, those that are aroused by pleasure and pain, and those that are required to defend oneself against danger, we are especially liable to emotional disorders of two types, those of disordered desire and those of disordered fear. Of these two, disordered fear is in a way the more fundamental, since it arises from our need for security, for self-preservation. Children who are neglected or abused, who suffer the loss of those who love and care for them, who are sickly, or in other ways feel insecure come into an unfriendly world and may suffer from excessive fear and anxiety. Such fears can become so overpowering as to be irrational and neurotic and ultimately take on a paranoic form.

A special problem of this type which spiritual directors often encounter is that of the scrupulous person who finds great difficulty in making moral decisions, and is always fearful that he or she is about to commit or has committed serious sins. Alphonse de Carera, O.P., wrote a pastoral work, *Scruples and Their Remedies*, as early as 1597. This pathology of the conscience is now recognized to be a variety of obsessive-compulsive neurosis and is caused by an excessive state of emotional anxiety which the scrupulous person is unable to control. What is typical of this condition is that the scrupulous person experiences great temporary relief from the reassurances of the confessor or director, but very quickly becomes anxious again. Unfortunately this pattern becomes a vicious circle in which the reassurance which is sought tends to reinforce the anxiety which clamors for reassurance.

Often beginners who are just becoming conscious of their own moral defects and are striving to do better go through brief attacks of scruples that usually can be handled adequately by the confessor or director. But if the pattern persists and becomes chronic, then expert assistance becomes necessary to break the pattern and discover the underlying half-conscious sources of anxiety.

The classical treatment of scruples was to insist that the victim rely on the judgment of the confessor or director and obey them absolutely. The scrupulous were not permitted to confess or to seek reassurances frequently, but only at proper times, in order to avoid the vicious circle of reinforcement just mentioned. This classical treatment remains sound, but can greatly be assisted today by the use of drugs that lower the anxiety-level and by techniques of "desensitization," etc., through which the victim learns to cope with anxiety attacks. When the director and the therapist are able to work together, this can be very effective. In such cases the role of the director or confessor is chiefly to encourage the victim to undergo therapy and to help them see that this is consistent with Christian principles.

But there is an opposite problem, the problem of what used to be called the "lax conscience" and today is often called "psychopathic personality." Such persons seem oblivious to the harmful consequences of their acts, lack empathy with the victims of their wrong acts, and exhibit little fear or guilt in the face of the consequences. Of course, not a few adolescents fit this description due to their lack of experience and their thoughtlessness, but they soon learn better. On the contrary, the psychopath seems fixed in this state of adolescent irresponsibility. A spiritual director dealing with an adult client who seems to have such a lax conscience, needs to gradually help them grow in self-awareness and empathy. Often the wakening of their imaginative and emotional life through literature and film, and the sharing of experiences with others can be of help. But if the condition is serious it requires expert psychological help and is often resistant to therapy.

The other aspect of our aggressive drives through which persons seek security from fear is the search for power, by which they can crush whatever seems to threaten them. One can seek power in order to be creative, constructive of what is good, but this aggressive drive can also become a tendency to be destructive, violent, hate-filled. It can even be turned against the self, so as to be self-destructive, a suicidal death-wish. At the opposite extreme, of course, are the timid or cowardly persons who wilt at every difficulty, and cling in dependency on others, and who always blame others for their failures. More insidious still, is the tendency to regard all authority figures as threats and to constantly rebel against every effort at guidance or correction. Thus some persons are filled with anger, often concealed or denied, which is irrationally misplaced because it has never been constructively channeled. Outrage at real injustice is, of course, justified, but at fancied injustice is paranoic.

Besides these pathologies related to aggressive emotions, are the disorders of desire. We need not only to be secure, but also to be happy, to find joy in life, and this means to love and be loved. Many children are deprived of the love they need, either through neglect or through constant criticism and correction, without receiving deserved praise. They believe themselves unlovable and that their own love will always be rejected. Life without love seems empty and meaningless. No wonder, then, that as they grow up their drives for sexual pleasure or for other sensual pleasures become compulsive, and even distorted in bizarre, "kinky" ways which they must pretend are normal and for which they clamor for public approval. Finally, it should be noted that the aggressive and pleasure seeking drives can become curiously intertwined, as in the sadistic and masochistic impulses where sexual pleasure is sought through suffering or inflicting pain.

Problems of gender identity are often met with in spiritual direction today and there is by no means general agreement as to how to deal with them. A distinction is commonly made between biological sex and gender which is a social construct, that is, the stereotype of what in a given culture it is to be a "real man" or a "real woman." Today the question is raised whether heterosexuality is simply a matter of gender and since a significant part of our population (perhaps 3 percent) are homosexual or bisexual in orientation, whether it would not be more humane to change our cultural stereotypes to make room for alternative constructs of gender.

Christian anthropology, however, has always maintained, and with solid grounds in the Bible and tradition, as well as in biology and psychology, that God created men and women for family life and therefore intended all humans to be heterosexual. The division of our race into "gays" and "straights" is itself a cultural construct intended to legitimate exclusive homosexuality. In fact, the population exhibits a range of variation from the heterosexual norm, just as it does from most norms. The causes for these deviations are only imperfectly known at present, but they probably include both genetic and developmental or learned factors which hinder the attainment of the norm of mature heterosexuality. Such defects in normal human development are to be attributed to natural causes, which if there had been no sin, God would have providentially prevented and which are theologically to be explained by the doctrine of original sin.

Thus persons seeking spiritual guidance who find themselves to be imperfectly heterosexual, and hence to some degree homosexual or bisexual need first of all to be assisted, as part of their growth in self-understanding, to face the fact of their condition honestly and without denial, simply for what it is, an incapacity to form normal heterosexual relations, with the probable result that their sexual drives tend to seek other outlets.

For Christian morality, however, genital satisfaction, both internal and external, was made for marriage and the family and must be achieved only there. Hence, spiritual directors cannot responsibly condone other forms of sexual activity. Their aim should be rather to assist persons with such problems to live a chaste celibate life. If it is possible for the person to obtain psychotherapy aimed at possible heterosexual development, or at least an anxiety-free adjustment to living as a celibate, this should be encouraged, and some psychotherapists report considerable success for such treatment.

Some bisexual persons can be encouraged to marry if they have learned consistent self-control. Otherwise, and what at present seems to be the majority of cases, for homosexuals to marry is irresponsible and they must face a life of celibacy. They are like those of whom Jesus spoke when he said, "Some are incapable of marriage because they were born so; some because they were made so by others; some, because they have renounced marriage for the sake of the kingdom of heaven. Whoever can accept this ought to accept it" (Mt 19:12). Indeed, such a celibate vocation, for whatever reason it be chosen, is not easy, yet by the grace of God it can be accepted and can become a means to the person's salvation. The Christian homosexual celibate can make of his or her disability for marriage an opportunity for friendship and for service of others. It is mistaken to argue, as some have done, that since celibacy requires a special charism, it is impossible for homosexuals who have no such charism to be chastely celibate. The fact of homosexuality, like other serious disabilities, is part of an individual's personal vocation and is thus never lacking in the grace to live it.

What then if the director finds that some he guides insist they cannot accept this traditional Christian view of sexuality, but believe that through committed, loving homosexual relationships they can be assisted to follow Christ? In my opinion a director should deal very sensitively with such persons who in our culture may be quite sincere in their convictions, but should gradually help them through study and prayer come to a truer understanding of their condition and the Christian answer to it. In all probability their own experience of the fragility of most such relationships will soon disillusion them and lead them to seek a true understanding. I would also want to emphasize the importance for the Christian community to assist single people, whether homosexual or not, to live a rich life of friendship and to foster the great help that support groups such as "Courage" can provide.

The ultimate remedy for all these disordered tendencies is to be found in union with God in whom alone there is total security and absolute assurance of acceptance and love. Unfortunately, however, precisely because we instinctively realize that God is the true answer to all our needs, emotional disorders can often express themselves in a false religiosity. Spiritual directors soon learn that what appears to be religious zeal may be a mask for an aggressive drive to control and dominate; what appears to be humility masks a desire to be praised; what appears to be obedience is really smoldering anger and resentment; what appears to be piety is compulsive scrupulosity; what appears to be a concern for orthodoxy is really paranoia; what appears to be religious devotion is covert sexual sensuality; what appears to be docility to direction is really dependency. The step-by-step exposure of these masks of religiosity, like Jesus' exposure of the Pharisees, is a painful process.

Other psychological pathologies of a still more serious character which often have physiological roots can only be mentioned here. The chief of these are: (a) schizoid tendencies which need to be suspected in persons who report visions, voices, demonic attacks, or whose thinking seems bizarre, and whose emotional responses are inappropriate; (b) manic-depressive tendencies to euphoria and depression; (c) hysteria, excessive emotionalism, excessive demands for attention, etc. These are part of the psychological frailty and vulnerability of human beings. Persons who suffer from them are hindered from devoting their full energies to spiritual growth, but under proper direction can learn to make these disabilities the occasion of spiritual progress through patience, trust in God, compassion for others. None of us are completely free from neurotic and even psychotic tendencies any more than we are free of physical ailments.

Asceticism

A question that spiritual directors who are studying the classics of spirituality and know something of modern psychology cannot help but ask is: *Why did the saints lay such emphasis on penance and self-mortification? Was this sado-masochism?* The answer of course is, "Yes, sometimes it was." That is why God tells St. Catherine when she requests him to let her suffer for his sake, the church, and the order, that she must understand that not suffering and penance, but love of God and neighbor is the goal of spirituality. "You asked for suffering, and you asked me to punish you for the sins of others. What you were not aware of was that you were, in effect, asking for love and light and knowledge of the truth."[49] This point is frequently made by Dominican spiritual writers. Thus Bl. Jordan wrote to Bl. Diana D'Andolo to moderate the penances she was practicing lest they hurt her health, and it is related of Bl. Henry Suso, in *The Life of the Servant*, written by his friend the Dominican nun Elisabeth Stagel, that after he had tortured himself in the most frightful ways he fell into a depression, and God showed him a very different way of purification.[50] Moreover, asceticism was always regarded as a means not the end, the single end of union with God. Thus Eckhart says:[51]

> Why do we pray, why do we fast, why do we do all our works, why are we baptized, why (most important of all) did God become man? I would answer, in order that God may be born in the soul and the soul be born in God. For that reason all the Scriptures were written, for that reason God created the world and all things.

It must be a concern of spiritual directors not to permit their clients to engage in penitential practices that are inappropriate to their health, age, occupation, and other responsibilities, and to correct morbidly masochistic or sadistic tendencies. Thus at the very beginning of the order, Bl. Jordan of Saxony, writing to the Sisters of St. Agnes at Bologna, [52]

> She who walks goes forward with moderation; she does not wander aimlessly, through negligence; nor does she rush on headlong with imprudent rashness and impetuosity. This latter is certainly the one I fear most for you: that some among you may indeed run without prudence or moderation, with excessive shedding of tears, immoderate vigils, fasting, or other similar austerities ill fitted to your feeble strength of body, for indeed you are not as robust as you would like to think, and one or other of you might easily be in reality completely exhausted even while thinking she still had great reserves of strength.

Yet the fact remains that all the canonized Dominican saints have practiced penance in a high degree, and many of them in extraordinary ways. St. Dominic, for example, kept vigil night after night, often scourging himself to blood; kept a severe Lenten fast from the feast of the Holy Cross, September 14th until Easter, never ate meat, walked barefoot on his long journeys, etc. St. Luis Beltrán engaged in similar penances, as did St. Margaret of Hungary, and especially St. Rose of Lima and St. Martin de Porres, etc. The primitive Dominican Constitutions prescribed a severely ascetic life for both men and women. Today much of this has been left to the individual discretion of members of the order, and it must be admitted that such practices are now uncommon. St. Rose of Lima, Patron of the Americas, in the spirit of prophecy exhorts us as follows:[53]

> Our Lord and Savior lifted up his voice and said with incomparable majesty: "Let all know that grace comes after tribulation. Let them know that without the burden of afflictions it is impossible to reach the height of grace. Let them know that gifts of grace increase as the struggles increase. Let men take care not to stray and be deceived. This is the only true stairway to paradise, and without the Cross they can find no road to climb to heaven."

Among the forms of asceticism commonly practiced in the order such as fasting and abstinence, "custody of the eyes," wearing of coarse clothing, and vigils, long prescribed in the Constitutions of the order, but now largely left to individual discretion, the general chapters frequently spoke of "the most holy law of silence" and of the cloister as its safeguard. Silence was the "mother of eloquence," especially needed in an order of preachers, teachers, and controversialists. St. Dominic was said to have "spoken only of God or to God." Often St. Peter Martyr was depicted over the cloister door, with his finger at his lips reminding the brethren of this "holy law" and in the fifteenth century Dominic Cavalca wrote the two little treatises, based on chapter 3 of the Epistle of St. James, on the bad and good deeds we commit in speech, *The Wounding Tongue*, and *The Fruits of the Tongue*. St. Vincent Ferrer wrote, [54]

> One may speak sometimes, if some necessity requires it, or if it is demanded by love of one's neighbor, or by obedience; and then thoughtfully and with few words, in a humble and quiet voice. Which one also ought to do when he has to answer a question about some matter. Yet for the edification of one's neighbors one should be silent for a moment so that by being silent one may learn how one should speak when the time comes

for him to speak, praying God that God himself will answer, by more interiorly inspiring in the hearts of one's neighbors the reply which meanwhile one abstains from giving, mastering his tongue by silence.

The Dominican habit, originally the white garment (plus a scapular, a sign of the Blessed Virgin's protection, and a black cloak, the sign of their itinerant mission) worn by the canons to whom Dominic had first belonged, was a symbol of poverty because of the coarse material of which it was made. It was intended to be a constant reminder to the friars and nuns and to others that the Dominicans had "left all things" to follow Christ. To wear the habit was at the same time a mark of honor and a humiliation, a "counter-cultural protest." Times have changed, and some feel today, that to dress like everyone else, to disappear in the crowd is the more humble thing to do. It is not easy to decide.

But perhaps the greatest means of purification for a Dominican is the one of which Jesus spoke when he said sadly and ironically, "I have come to bring not peace but the sword" (Mt 10:34), that is, the conflicts inevitably caused by preaching the word of truth. In the thirteenth century, Raymund of Peñafort, addressing the friars as Master of the Order wrote, [55]

> The two-edged sword [of the Word, Heb 4:12. Rv 1:16, 2:12, 19:15] consists in conflict without, fears within. It falls with double or treble force within, when the cunning spirit troubles the depths of your heart with guile and enticements. You have learned enough already about these kinds of warfare, or you would not have been able to enjoy peace and interior tranquillity in all its beauty. The sword falls with double and treble force externally when, without cause being given, there breaks out from within the church persecution in spiritual matters, where wounds are more serious, especially when inflicted by friends. This is the enviable and blessed cross of Christ.

What is the meaning of asceticism (from the Greek for "discipline")? While it is sometimes said that Judaism is not an ascetic religion, in fact the strict practice of the law with its dietary prescriptions, its fasts, washing, times of prayer, and its nazarite vows, imposes a high degree of asceticism on the devout. While John the Baptist practiced an even stricter asceticism, Jesus and the apostles did not do so during his public life because they were constantly occupied with the exhausting demands of the ministry, yet they lived in poverty and danger.

Asceticism has a threefold purpose: (1) to discipline one's human faculties to bring them under control of the will and thus to restore the integrity of the person which original and actual sin have undermined; (2) to acknowledge one's debt to justice for one's actual sins and the harm they have done to oneself and to others; (3) to unite oneself with Jesus in his passion in reparation for the sins of the whole world and for the conversion of others.

Even the first of these values is not understood by many in our society where the pursuit of pleasure is considered true happiness; yet most people recognize that athletes have to undergo a training which is very strict. While directors need to see that the client makes use of such discipline but with moderation, it is especially the other two values that require careful explanation if they are to make sense today.

To understand them we must ask why God willed that Jesus suffer on the cross? This is often explained, as it was by the great St. Anselm, by saying that Jesus had to pay the debt of sin which we sinners owed to God the Father. While it is true that St. Paul sometimes uses this language of "vicarious atonement" and that it is found in many spiritual writers, including Dominican ones, it is not very satisfying intellectually, and to many today seems to portray God not as a loving Father, but as revengeful God who demands his pound of flesh.

If one reads Aquinas attentively, however, one finds a deeper meaning for Jesus' sacrificial death. God sent his Son to reveal to us that God is love, so that we might turn back from the sin that is destroying us and our world and allow God to forgive and heal us. If we had received him Jesus would not have needed to die, but in fact we sinners killed Jesus on the cross—it was we who killed him not God. Why then did the Father permit this since he must have known it would happen? God the Father permitted it and Jesus accepted death not because the Father demanded justice for his own satisfaction, but in order that God's Son might give the ultimate proof that God himself loves us so much that he is willing to die for us in his own Son who also is God. Only when we see this will we believe that God is love and repent our sins.

Why then do the Bible and tradition sometimes use the language of "payment for sin"? Because, once again, it is not God who demands punishment of the sinner but we humans. God is always ready to forgive and, as it were, forget the demands of justice. But if God were to allow sin to go unpunished, the human victims of sin would cry out that God is not just, and those who are ready to commit sin would say, "God doesn't care!" Therefore, that we may never forget what harm sin does, God requires that it be punished, yet out of love of us he has taken on himself, in the person of his Son, in whom the Father lives, as an earthly father lives in his children and suffers in them, the punishment that is due sin. Thus understood the cross is always a revelation of love, never of revenge.

In the light of this understanding of the cross it becomes understandable why St. Catherine and other Dominican saints actually prayed that they might suffer with Jesus, and why they took on themselves ascetic practices that helped them share in his passion. They hungered fully to realize the guilt of their own sins that they might be utterly converted from them, and they thirsted to prove the unselfishness of their love for Jesus and to make reparation for the sins of others that they might be converted and live.

There is a mystery in this thirst of the saints to be one with Jesus on the cross, not because like masochists they take pleasure in suffering, but because they suffer not to be able to relieve his suffering. It is like the feeling of a mother at the bedside of a sick child who wishes that it was she not the child who had to endure the pain. In the paintings of the Bl. Fra Angelico we see St. Dominic seated at the foot of the cross in silent meditation, and St. Thomas Aquinas is traditionally reported to have said that he learned more from the cross than from books.

Today it is often said that instead of fasting and scourging, the modern asceticism is the hardships of the ministry, the hours of study, the endless meetings, the patient endurance of the clash of opinions of our times, the long hours, the sharing of the lot of the poor, the contempt of secular society, and often the dangers of persecution in totalitarian states and in war, and so on. There is much truth in this, yet how is one to have the courage for all this without deliberately taking on smaller penances?

It would seem to me that spiritual directors today should teach the following principles: (a) Christians must practice at least the penances required by the church, its fasts, abstinence, vigils, holidays, the penances given in the confessional as these are compatible with health and work, and not seek to omit them or simply reduce them to meaningless formalities; (b) Christians must also take upon themselves certain regular penances fitted to correct their own particular faults, especially during the Advent and Lenten seasons. These additional practices should be approved by the spiritual director in order to assure that they are prudent. (c) As Christians meet the hardships and losses of life, they must accept them in a spirit of confidence in God's love and in union with Jesus and the Mater Dolorosa, and the director should support and console them in this grieving process. (d) As Christians advance in the spiritual life and draw closer to Jesus their desire to suffer in reparation for the sins of others is certain to increase as their compassion for the world increases. Directors should not discourage this, but should try to help the client free this desire from whatever may be morbid, masochistic, or self-dramatizing in it.

Passive Purification

Ascetic practices voluntarily undertaken are helpful only when appropriate, and the practitioner (and even the director) may very well be mistaken about what is appropriate, because the sinfulness that needs purification has a way of blinding the sinner to the perception of his or her own sin. Consequently, the deeper purification of the person requires the action of God which must be accepted in patience and gratitude, as one submits to a surgeon. Although it was not until John of the Cross and the Carmelite school of spirituality that the ancient experience of mystics of the spiritual "night" received its clearest formulation. Yet as St. John says,[56] it is biblically portrayed in vivid terms in the Book of Job, the Psalms, on which Aquinas commented, and the Canticle of Canticles on which he was said to have also written a commentary now lost. St. Catherine herself underwent an extraordinary "night of the spirit" in her last days as indicated in her writings and her biography by St. Raymond of Capua.[57]

John of the Cross clearly distinguishes the "night of the soul" from the "night of the spirit" and sees these as transitions from the purgative to the illuminative and from the illuminative to the unitive way, respectively. In terms of Aquinas' anthropology on which St. John's own paradigm is based, there are two levels of the human psyche that require special purification, the level of sensitive life, and the level of intellectual life. The first is that of the bodily exterior and interior senses and drives, the second that of the spiritual intelligence and will.

Those who are devoted to the practice of prayer first have to struggle with the hubbub of external sensations and the vagaries of the imagination and memory, and with the tumult of their feelings. While at times these sensations and feelings support their prayer and lead to "consolations," pleasant inner experiences, they also very often are simply distractions. Many beginners say that they are so distracted they find prayer difficult and come to content themselves with a few hurried vocal prayers. They are really the victims of the outside world around them and of their own busyness. The director, therefore, has to show them why they are distracted and how they might become more recollected by finding a time and place of quiet, perhaps before the blessed sacrament, by spiritual reading, by participation in the liturgy, etc., in short the "arts of prayer." With a refreshing realism the English Dominican Bede Jarrett said to those who claimed they could not pray because of the distractions of their busy lives:[58]

It was all very well for Peter and the others to go up to the hills and to say, "It is good for us to be here." The untroubled beauty of the still air, perfectly serene, is wonderful. To appreciate and enjoy it is all very well for the moment. But it is not life....We were given the faith, not to do nothing, but to work with it and for it and to pray until He comes. It is true that we are given our mysteries with a clear knowledge of them that is withheld from the world; but we were given them that we might work and live, not rest. Heaven is our resting place. Here, we must work till we die. He climbed the hills, indeed, our Blessed Master, once or twice to get a rest between his labors. But even the hills were no place of resting for Him, except when on a hill in utter agony He died. Work is our portion and not leisure, not way of ease, not the lifting of temptation, not a prayer that all the busy-ness may cease...He came to bring not peace but the sword. The life He came to teach could be lived in the market place, a busy life, in warfare, not all in shirking the busy toil of men. It is very natural to long for quiet of course, but to give in to it is a misunderstanding what the incarnation means.

Gradually the Christian in whatever vocation achieves the ability to pray with some degree of recollection. In the Dominican tradition one of the most appropriate ways to do this is by the recitation, or still better the singing, of the liturgical hours. The psalms express in a profoundly human way the role of the senses, the imagination, the memory, the feelings in prayer. The rosary, with its loving repetition and its tactile fingering of the beads, was originally devised as a substitute for the Hours for the illiterate, and when it is said with a serious attempt to meditate on the mysteries of the life of Jesus with Mary, "who remembered all these things, pondering them in her heart," it is the perfect way to learn meditative prayer.

Eventually, however, the imaginative pleasure and emotional fantasy of this type of prayer tends to lose its charm. On the purely natural, psychological plane this is nothing more than the fact that all imaginative and emotional experiences become routine. The element of grace, however, is that as one meditates habitually, a deeper level of the soul begins to awaken, and makes these superficial impressions and feelings less and less meaningful. A hunger for something much deeper and more intimate emerges. It is this entrance with Jesus into the desert where the transient attractions of this world can no longer satisfy, that is the "dark night of the soul," that is, of sense life that is now taking place.

As we shall see, this does not mean that the process of purification is complete. Far from it, for that process will go deeper and deeper to the very end of the journey! What it means is that something more positive than mere purification is now emerging and in the illuminative stage will come to predominate. A special aspect of Christian asceticism is the vigil or "waiting for the Lord" which the early Christians felt so keenly, since their expectation of his coming soon was so vivid in their minds. It has been preserved in the liturgy by the great Easter Vigil and is recommended for other feasts in the Sacramentary and Liturgy of the Hours. Old age is especially marked by this "waiting for the Lord," which should not be a time of depression and inactivity, but of a lively, hope-filled waiting for the Beloved. Yet such loving waiting is itself a purification and those who give spiritual direction to the elderly should help them to understand that their last years are by no means wasted.[59]

Baptism and Reconciliation

God's work of purifying the Christian from sin and its effects centers in three sacraments; baptism, reconciliation, and the anointing of the sick (the last of these is especially relevant to the end of the journey and will be discussed in our last chapter). The spiritual director must ask the beginner: "Have you meditated on what the fact that you are a baptized Christian means for your life? How do you use the sacrament of reconciliation to keep the life of baptism flourishing in you?

Baptism is the beginning of the journey, the sacrament of the new creation, the birth into the life of grace, the setting out on the journey to God. It is not merely, or even chiefly, a purification from sin, but rather the infusion of new life, yet it is, and in the most fundamental way, such a purification. It wipes out not only original sin, but all sin, yet not all the effects of sin in the form of the evil tendencies ("concupiscence") which remain within us. Why does it not remove all these effects of sin? Because God wishes us as free persons to cooperate in our own work of sanctification. Only Mary and Jesus, among all members of our race, were free from the first moment of their existence from all intrinsic effects of sin, as the flowers of Israel and of the whole human family which had been prepared by God for ages to begin the promised reign of God; but they, too, had to struggle in life against the extrinsic effects of sin.

Aquinas hesitated to agree to the view that Mary was without original sin, because it seemed to imply that she did not need to be redeemed by Christ, although he realized she must have been purified from all sin before being able to give her consent on behalf of Israel and all humanity to Christ's birth. Following the insight of the Franciscan friar, Bl. Duns Scotus, the church saw that Mary was indeed redeemed by Christ by a preventive redemption so that she might be the New Eve with him, the New Adam.

Aquinas also puzzled over the doctrine that baptism is necessary to salvation. What then becomes of the countless millions that have not heard of Christ or of baptism? What becomes of unbaptized children? St. Thomas' answer to the first question was that the grace of Christ is not limited to baptism and hence that all who do good as they know it, do so because the grace of Christ has enabled them to choose God implicitly (as we have seen for children in their first human act). How does this grace of Christ reach them? Aquinas said simply that perhaps it might come through an angel! Since Vatican II we can admit that this grace can come through other religions in which at least a trace of God's revelation of himself to humanity is present, mediated also by the prayers of the church for the salvation of all.[60]

As regards unbaptized children, Aquinas recognized they had committed no personal sin and therefore deserved no personal punishment, yet concluded that since the grace of Christ was not mediated to them they could not attain the beatific vision, but only some form of natural happiness ("limbo", the "threshold of heaven"). A great commentator of Aquinas, Cardinal Cajetan suggested that the prayers of the parents and the church might mediate Christ's grace to them and thus anticipate baptism.

Today, it seems perfectly Thomistic to say: (a) Since how God's will to save all humankind reaches beyond the church has not been revealed to us, we can only speculate about it, but with confidence that God's mercy is far greater than we can imagine; (b) Israel and the New Israel of the church were chosen by God to be his visible instruments to bring the grace of Christ to all, yet the prayers of the faithful and the grace of Christ extend to all the world.

Thus in the case of the child brought to baptism, we need not suppose that until that moment the child has been under Satan's power. Rather, the prayers of the parents and the church have begun to draw the child into the path that leads to God even at the moment of its conception (as occurred in the most perfect way for Mary and her Son) and that the sacrament of baptism is only the public completion of a long hidden process. Similarly, for the adult, the process of conversion and Christian initiation is a long one, completed in adult baptism, confirmation, and eucharistic communion. Finally, the same thing is true of the sacrament of reconciliation; penitents before they come to confession have already been touched by the grace of Christ and have begun their conversion or they would not come to the sacrament at all.

This last point provides an answer to a problem that today many spiritual directors, who are not priests, experience. They work with clients, form a relationship where the clients open up to them and confess their sins; yet the director who is not a priest cannot give them absolution, but must tell them to wait and go to a priest whom they may not know and with whom they will have to make a painful confession all over again, perhaps to a confessor who does not understand them as well as the director. In my opinion this difficulty shows a lack of understanding of the meaning of the sacrament of reconciliation, which is not simply a private act but an ecclesial one.

In the early church serious sins were confessed publicly so that the absolution was clearly an act of forgiveness by God mediated through the Christian community under the headship of its priest. The spiritual director to whom someone confesses sin should assure them that God has already accepted their conversion, but that for this to be complete and confirmed by sacramental grace, they need to make amends to those they have offended, and especially to the whole Christian community by going to the priest who is authorized to represent Christ in that community to ask for his and the community's forgiveness. Mercifully, the community today will not demand public confession, but it will require private confession to the representative of Christ in his church. The spiritual director who is not a priest ought not to claim that she or he has a right to speak for the community, as a priest does, and the client should be helped to see that the delay and pain of going to confession is part of the conversion process.

The sacrament of reconciliation is to be understood as a renewal of baptism, helpful for the struggle against venial sins, and essential for the restoration of the union with God in grace when that has been lost by mortal sin. The spiritual director is not necessarily the confessor, but should be of help to the penitent in the regular use of this great sacrament which, since Vatican II, quite contrary to the intentions of the council, has become much neglected. It must not be a routine, but ought to be regular and should be directed precisely toward an ever deeper interior conversion. The fundamental question one must ask oneself in preparation for the sacrament is, "How have my actions brought me closer to God, my neighbor, and my true self as God's image, or how they led me to forget God, and harm my neighbor and myself?" The recalling of the commandments and laws of the church are very helpful in this examination, but should not be central to it, since they are only rules that point to the goals of Christian life, not the goals themselves which are the union with God and neighbor in honest love.

The director, in helping those he guides, should be sure that they neither presume on God's mercy by taking their sins lightly, nor waste time and energy by brooding over forgiven sins, but should rather make their sins the occasion of a more genuine conversion and God's mercy the reason for an increase in love. As Bede Jarrett, O.P., said in a sermon after speaking of the great mercy of God:[61]

> I must not take as my conclusion that it does not matter that I sin, for God will forgive me. God will not forgive me if I am not sorry for my sins, and sorrow I cannot have if I take no trouble to avoid sin and merely think of the infinity of God's mercy. But the way it should affect me is this: I should try to make capital out of this past sin by letting it bring me nearer to God. We know that he is so powerful that he could have prevented sin. We know that he did not prevent sin. We know, therefore, that sin must some way fit into his plan. Let us say, as St. Augustine did, that God is so powerful that he can bring good out of evil....Sin, then, can be used afterwards to make the memory of it an inspiration towards a greater love of God. This is also the real act of sorrow, the perfect contrition that thinks of sin and is sorry for it because it has offended God. Here is true sorrow in which self is forgotten and God only remembered. It is not sorrow only, but sweet sorrow; it is love.

=================

Chapter 6

The Process of Illumination

Illumination and Virtue

Purification from sin is only the negative aspect of the positive process of spiritual growth, and that growth means the development of a mature Christian character which will enable us regularly and consistently to act as Jesus Christ did. Spiritual directors, therefore, should never suppose that clients are really being converted from sin just because they seem not to be doing what is wrong. Purification cannot take place without illumination, without the development of positive behavior and the virtues that make it consistent. Directors must therefore constantly return to the question: *What are you doing in the service of God and neighbor?* God said to St. Catherine that she could serve him only by serving her neighbor.

The classical term "illumination" seems a little puzzling here. As mentioned before, it derives from Origen and the early Alexandrian school of catechesis, which in turn derived it, on the one hand, from the gospel of St. John and its metaphor of "light" for grace; and on the other hand, from Neoplatonic philosophy which used the metaphor of the radiation of the sun for the emanation of all reality from the One. Consequently, the sacrament of baptism was called "illumination" in the Eastern church, since it was the bestowal of the life of grace. Hence, the process of "illumination" is the process of growth in grace, in depth of spiritual life. One can think of a plant flourishing and bearing fruit by the energy that comes to it from the illumination of the sun.

This growth in grace is a growth in virtues, in our mature abilities to respond to God's call and move forward steadily on our journey to him. The word "virtue" (and the biblical Greek *arete* which it translates) means etymologically, "the ability to act like a man." This is no doubt

118

androcentric, but it is not so much sexist as it is based on the simple admiration for the physical strength and courage of mature men. Hence, the idea is one of power, the ability to do what is difficult. For Aquinas, therefore, a "virtue" is the power to overcome a difficulty, and it is reasonable to suppose that God has endowed human persons with as many such powers as there are basic difficulties in human life.

The Organism of the Virtues

Our natural virtues, however, although God-given, must be acquired (the "acquired virtues") by a natural learning process. By dealing with the basic problems of life we learn by trial and error and with help of the guidance of others who have already acquired these virtues to overcome life's difficulties, and by repeated acts achieve the trained ability which is a virtue. Ability to deal with one type of problem, however, does not equip us to deal with other types of problems, so that we need many specific virtues, and all these must somehow be harmonized and unified, so that by training we become able to meet all situations in an appropriate and flexible way with the right combination of skills. This formation of character produces what we can compare to a healthy physical organism and call it the organism of the virtues.

These acquired virtues, however, are not sufficient for the Christian. Since our goal transcends our human nature, our virtues must be transformed by grace and empowered to reach that higher goal. This transformation of our acquired virtues results in the infused virtues (given by the Holy Spirit). Just as our natural and supernatural ends should not be thought of as parallel, since the natural end is transformed and taken up into the supernatural end, so our infused virtues should not be imagined as a second set of virtues parallel to the acquired ones, but as transformations of the acquired virtues, "grace perfecting nature."

The infused virtues are given in conversion and baptism, since they are the work of grace. But what happens if the person is a newly baptized child, or an adult who has just been converted but has never acquired these virtues or who even has acquired vices? This is a theological puzzle which has never been fully solved. In my opinion the answer is probably to be found in the fact that grace heals and elevates nature only gradually and not without the cooperative effort of the recipient of grace.

If we think of a convert who is in the habit of drinking too much, we should not expect that baptism will at once remove his alcoholism. When it does (as it sometimes does) we are witnessing a moral miracle! What baptism gives him is the firm commitment to God and the resolution to strive to overcome his vice. Moreover, the infused virtue of temperance begins to operate in him (although imperfectly) to enable him to resist temptation and to find the means to do so (such as joining Alcoholics Anonymous). If he keeps up this struggle, continues proper treatment, prays, and uses the sacraments, his infused virtue will sustain him in overcoming his vice and acquiring the natural virtue of temperance which it will also transform in relation to his commitment to God.

From this analysis two things are clear: (a) We ought not to rely on our infused virtues given in baptism as if we do not have to practice the natural virtues, even if we sometimes fail; (b) The infused virtues are a real empowerment in helping us acquire these natural virtues as well as transforming them into effective means to our supernatural goal.

Aquinas, as St. Augustine before him, attempted to correlate the various passages of scripture which enumerate the virtues, but he also tried to show that this enumeration was not merely arbitrary but had systematic roots in human psychology and in the basic life problems which must be solved on our spiritual journey. Without claiming that this Thomistic schema is definitive, I present it as a very penetrating and helpful model of Christian character to which a director can refer in trying to understand the strengths and weaknesses of a client at any given moment of human development.

First we must distinguish between a disposition to virtue and a mature virtue. A disposition is the psychological beginning of a real virtue and may be present either as a feature of a person's individual temperament (e.g., some persons are by temperament more inclined to gentleness, to courage, to insight, than others) or as the first steps in the acquisition of a virtue. Then we must distinguish the intellectual virtues which enable a person to use their intelligence effectively in gaining knowledge from the moral virtues which without qualification make the person a good person, able to attain happiness in God.

Furthermore, we must distinguish the moral virtues which deal with the means toward the goal of our life from the theological virtues (faith, hope, and love, mentioned by St. Paul in 1 Cor 13; cf. Rm 5:1–2) which unite the Christian to that very goal, to God. Then we must relate to these virtues the fruits of the Spirit (mentioned by St. Paul, "love, joy, patience, kindness, generosity, faithfulness, gentleness, self-control" (Gal 5:22–23). Then, we must distinguish among these fruits of the Spirit certain ones of supreme excellence, the beatitudes (listed by Jesus at the beginning of the Sermon on the Mount, Mt 5:3–10, "Blessed are the poor," etc.).

Finally, we must add to all these the Seven Gifts of the Holy Spirit (derived from Is 7:2–3a in the LXX and Rev 5:6) which, according to Aquinas, do not add new objects to the other virtues but transform their mode from the merely human mode of acting to a participation in God's "graceful" way of acting under the inspiration of the Holy Spirit.

This formidable array of virtues is interrelated and unified in a remarkable organic fashion. Since virtue enables us to live "according to reason," that is, in touch with reality and free from the illusions created by sin, the intellectual virtues, although they do not as such make us good human beings, are needed in order to guide our lives. Certain of these intellectual virtues deal with the understanding of the world as it is: the theoretical virtues, and these are three: (1) insight by which we understood the first principles of all knowledge directly from our experience; (2) science by which we reason from first principles to a detailed knowledge of reality; (3) wisdom by which we organize all that we have learned through the various sciences into a worldview.

These virtues, which we naturally acquire by hard study, are transformed by corresponding infused virtues and are given their divine mode by the gifts of the Holy Spirit of the same names (usually translated, "understanding, knowledge, and wisdom") and which produce the fruits such as the beatitude, "Blessed are the clean of heart, for they shall see God;" (insight) "Blessed are they who mourn, for they shall be comforted;" (science, because the knowledge of earthly things often makes us sad); and "Blessed are the peacemakers for they shall be called children of God" (wisdom brings unity and peace). The Dominican tradition has always seen the moral and intellectual virtues as distinct but intimately linked. As the encyclopedist of the thirteenth century, Vincent of Beauvais wrote in his work, *On the Education of Sons of the Nobility:*[62]

There are four qualities of wisdom which especially inspire anyone to discipline or study, namely, its dignity, delight, permanence, and usefulness....Just as he who ploughs and sows, first clears his field of thorns and thistles and then sows in the plowed earth, so he who wishes to achieve the doctrine of wisdom, should first plough the earth of his heart with diligence and extirpate the weeds of vice, and then he will be able to receive the word of truth, for wisdom cannot enter into a soul of bad will.

The practical intellectual virtues which enable us to think effectively about how we control ourselves and how we control the world, are prudence and art (technology), respectively. Aquinas thought that the arts, as such, pertain only to this world and hence are not as such transformed by grace, but prudence is so transformed, unifies all our practical knowledge, operates in a divine mode under the inspiration of the Holy Spirit through the gift of counsel, and produces the fruit of the beatitude, "Blessed are the merciful, for they shall receive mercy."

If we have learned to use our intelligence well to guide our lives, then we can acquire, and still need the moral virtues to regulate our desires and emotions. There are many such virtues as there are many desires, but since there are four main problems in life, as we shall see, there are our four main ("cardinal") moral virtues. The first of these is prudence as regards individual, family and social behavior, which we have already seen is a practical intellectual virtue, but which needs also to be grouped with the moral virtues, because we cannot think effectively about practical matters, unless our desires are under control. The second is justice, whether between individuals of the community to the individual members, or the members to the community, which enables us to transcend our self-centeredness so that we can also respect the rights of others. It is the great social virtue which is elevated by the gift of piety (*pietas* in Latin means piety as duty and respect for the dignity of others) and which bears the fruit of the beatitudes, and "Blessed are the meek, for they will possess the earth."

The last two cardinal virtues deal directly with the self-control of our emotions. One is moderation (or temperance) by which we control our desires for physical pleasure in food, drink, and sex, which can enslave us and darken our reason. Moderation takes on a divine mode by the gift of fear of the Lord and produces the fruit of the beatitude, "Blessed are the poor in spirit, for the kingdom of heaven is theirs." The other is courage (fortitude), whether in doing good deeds or risking one's possessions or in suffering great troubles and in enduring troubles for a long time, by which we control our aggressive tendencies. This virtue receives a divine mode from the gift of fortitude and produces the fruit of the beatitude, "Blessed are those who hunger and thirst after justice, for they will be satisfied."

Along with the four cardinal virtues Aquinas lists a multitude of lesser virtues, each of which most resembles some one of the cardinal virtues, but deal with problems of lesser difficulty. For example, the virtue of gratitude is grouped with the cardinal virtue of justice, because it is like justice in that it is a kind of repayment for the good done us by others, yet, unlike justice, gratitude does not oblige us to repay an exact equivalent of what we have been given. It may demand only a simple "Thank you." We are guided to these virtues by the ten commandments. Thus, the commandments of the first table of the law (the first three against idolatry, blasphemy, and work on the sabbath) correlate with the theological virtues, the others with the virtue of justice, but also the sixth and ninth pertain to temperance, the fifth to courage, the sixth and seventh to justice in special ways, and the fourth to prudence which requires that we are respectful toward the guidance of parents and other teachers.

As prudence gives intellectual guidance to all the moral virtues, so wisdom unifies all the intellectual virtues, and with love unifies the entire life of virtue. It is characteristic of Thomism that, while love is supreme in the moral order, it is joined with wisdom which is supreme in the intellectual order. Although Aquinas does not say so, I would add that we can correlate the moral and the theological virtues as follows: (a) prudence in the Old Testament is correlated with faith under the name of "wisdom," which is faith in practice; (b) justice, under the biblical name of "righteousness" goes with love which includes but surpasses justice; (c) fortitude and temperance, because they detach us from enslavement to worldly desires in view of heaven, are eschatological virtues and correlate with hope.

As Aquinas systematized the virtues he did the same for the corresponding vices; each virtue standing in the middle between unreasonable extremes of behavior which are vices. He also adopted from the desert fathers (by way of John Cassian's *Conferences* which were favorite reading for St. Dominic and his first disciples), the scheme of the seven deadly (or capital) Sins: lust, greed, anger, sloth, avarice, envy, and vanity, which are not necessarily the gravest sins, but which are the roots of other sins. This tradition is of practical importance in spiritual direction, since these are the common weak spots in human character. It is often useful to ask the persons we direct to try to identify their "predominant fault" which underlies their other failings and to focus their efforts in uprooting it, just as a physician avoids treating symptoms rather than the underlying disease.

Similarly, a director should help those he guides to build on their strong points. Luis of Granada, O.P., however, also warns directors against favoring some special virtue in their disciples to the neglect of the balance of the virtues in which a really sound character consists. He writes:[63]

> Each one, impelled by ignorance or unconscious pride, extols himself by commending the practices to which he is most given. Just as the savant will praise the science which is the object of his study, and depreciate the merit of all the rest. The orator will tell you that there is nothing comparable to eloquence; the astronomer, that there is nothing superior to the study of the heavenly bodies. In fact, the theologian, the linguist, the philosopher, the commentator, will each in his turn offer good reasons to prove the preeminence and incontestable superiority of the science he professes. Similar, though less open, is the struggle between the advocates of the different virtues; each one would have his method prevail over that of others, believing that as it has proved profitable to him, it must prove so to all. Hence arise unfavorable judgments upon the lives of others, divisions and disputes among the brethren.

Growth in Virtue

Too often Christians, although avoiding mortal sins, remain at a mediocre level of holiness, because of a failure to work at growth in virtue. A director must ask the question: *What are the strengths and weaknesses in virtue of these persons? Are they working to strengthen the weak spots in their character?*

At the beginning of the spiritual life when the task of purification is predominant, a Christian must practice a consistent asceticism to develop those cardinal virtues that bring one's own passions under control, moderation and courage. As Eckhart constantly emphasized (and here Catherine is in hearty agreement), detachment from the enslavement to pleasure (moderation) and the patience to endure suffering for the sake of virtue (courage) are the indispensable foundations of moral life. There is no greater illusion than to believe one can become Christlike while at the same time wasting one's energies on pleasures and fears that are unreasonable. For Eckhart this means total detachment from all that is created so that the Son of God can be born in the depths of the soul which has become entirely open to him:[64]

> There is a power in the mind which touches neither time nor flesh: it emanates from the spirit and remains in the spirit and is totally spiritual. In this power God is fully verdant and flowing, in all the joy and all the honor that he is in himself. There reigns such a dear joy, so incomprehensibly great a joy, that no one can ever fully speak of it. For in this power, the eternal Father is ceaselessly begetting his eternal Son, in such a way that this power begets the Son of God together with him, and begets itself as this selfsame Son in the identical power of the Father.

We cannot be open to God until we are emptied of our false self which has been created by pride, that false self-love which is the root of all sin, the sin to which Satan tempted the first parents. Pride is the refusal to subject oneself to God and to honestly admit one's own limitations and it blinds us to reality and leads us to live in a world of illusions created by our own unruly desires. Vanity, the excessive regard for others' approval, is one of the cardinal vices, but pride is something far more serious and is not reckoned as one of the seven cardinal sins because it is the root of all sin. The virtue which opposes it is a form of moderation, namely humility, which leads us to be content with even the least place in the scale of beings, if that is what we really are. All the spiritual writers point out that as pride is the root of all sin because it closes off grace, telling us we can achieve happiness without God's help, so humility is the foundation of all virtue, since it opens us up to the grace of God with whom all things are possible.

Hence the spiritual director should pay the greatest attention to whether the Christian is growing in humility, and should be quick to oppose every sign of pride. Today when pop psychology puts so much emphasis on the neurosis of "low self-regard" or "poor self-image," it is not easy to understand this classical emphasis on humility. Our democratic culture will hardly accept the idea that it may be a virtue to be content with anything but first place. Yet it is plain that Jesus Christ was humble and taught humility. "Amen, I say to you, unless you turn and become like children, you will not enter the kingdom of heaven. Whoever humbles himself like this child is the greatest in the kingdom of heaven" (Mt 18:3–4).

Psychologists are correct in believing that low self-esteem is often the result of the neglect of a community to encourage its members by due praise and support, but it can also be the result of an excessive appetite for attention and flattery (vanity). Some are also bitterly resentful because of their own defects rather than willing to admit them honestly and to work for their correction. Directors should seek to help those they guide to recognize with honest realism: (a) both their strengths and their weaknesses; (b) realize that their Christian dignity does not rest on whether they are "number 1" in any respect, but on the fact that they have their unique place in God's creation and his kingdom; (c) be willing to serve God and the community even in lowly capacities when this is needed by the common good.

They must also come to see that although the spiritual life is a long journey to perfect rest in God, yet by reason of faith, hope, and charity, the Christian is already present with God in eternity in every moment of their lives. To be united with God here and now requires no other justification. As Eckhart said so beautifully, "This I know. That the only way to live is like the rose which lives without a why."[65]

A story told of St. Thomas Aquinas illustrates this. One day one of the cooperator friars of a priory where he was staying was sent by the prior to beg in the streets for the community's daily food. According to the rule, the friar was required to take a companion with him, and meeting Thomas in the cloister, and not recognizing that he was a famous Master of Theology and a counselor of kings, asked him to come with him to beg. Thomas said nothing, but simply went along, leaving his own work behind. We also read of how St. Margaret of Hungary, a king's daughter, whose two sisters married kings, became a nun and always took on herself the unpleasant task of cleaning the fish for the other sisters, who treated her with contempt for smelling of fish. If begging or cleaning fish are needed for the community, what member of the community should think it beneath his or her dignity to perform that service?

But Aquinas also sees studiousness as a form of moderation, since it enables one to steer a mean between a neglect of the study needed by one's vocation and mere idle curiosity; and so also for meekness which moderates our aggressiveness, and clemency which moderates our disciplining of others under our care, and self-control our love of pleasure; while modesty in dress, decorum in gesture, and the ability to recreate well manifest this moderation in external behavior. It is in helping the beginner learn moderation that the director especially exercises the role of confrontation, exposing the weakness and rationalizations of the addict and pleasure lover.

No less important for spiritual freedom than moderation in pleasure is courage in continuing on the spiritual journey in spite of obstacles, striking a mean between passivity and cowardice on the one hand, and rash aggressiveness on the other. We are more likely to sin from too much love of pleasure than from too little (although phlegmatic and melancholic temperaments may be too cold); so we are more likely to sin from being too aggressive than from being too patient (although choleric and mercurial temperaments may be too hot). It is in helping the beginner learn patience and courage to continue that the spiritual director particularly exercises the role of support and encouragement.

Besides the supreme courage to risk death required of the soldier in war and the martyr in spiritual warfare, true courage requires magnanimity, the courage to risk failure in undertaking important good works; generosity to risk poverty in giving large sums for good works; patience in the hardships of life, long-suffering in enduring these hardships day after day.

Ministry

What is most proper to the illuminative phase, however, is not the virtues of self-control which should have been solidly implanted in the purgative phase, but the virtues of justice and prudence which are characteristic of the mature personality.

The human person is essentially communitarian and we exist not just for ourselves but for the common good to which we owe our service in return for the support it gives us. Jesus said, "The Son of Man did not come to be served, but to serve" (Mt 20:28). It is justice that moderates this service, enabling us to respect the rights of others and to give to them the service due to them in proper order.

Each of us owes our neighbor—first our family, and then society, especially those members of society who are most neglected, the debt of social justice, in a world where sins have led to war, crime, poverty, neglect. The "preferential option for the poor" of which Vatican II spoke, simply means that the Christian must follow Jesus in his special concern for those in a community whose needs are neglected, for the outcasts, the "little ones" not because they are somehow of more worth than others, but because no one else appreciates their equal worth as human beings. Jesus himself told us that we will be judged on whether we have recognized him, as a human, in the hungry, the sick, the imprisoned (Mt 25:31–46).

The spiritual director of those who hold public office, or who manage businesses on which the welfare of others depend, or of the military and police who maintain public order, or of professional people who provide essential services, have an especially difficult task in helping those they guide fulfill their roles for the common good and not for their own power. Directors are usually in no position to judge the decisions of such persons, but they must try to help them achieve a truly Christian vision of their responsibilities. What courage it took for the Dominican preachers like Antonio Montesinos and Bartolomé de las Casas (who had himself been a slave-holder) to refuse absolution to the Spanish colonists who refused to release the Native Americans they had unjustly enslaved!

The same goes for those who counsel persons engaged in the struggle for social reform, who are often well-intentioned but lacking in real expertise, or inclined to revolutionary violence, or to attacks on legitimate public and church authority. On the one hand, it is necessary to encourage their work for justice, often against great odds, and, on the other, to insist that they not be tempted to seek good ends by wrong and unlawful means.

Justice takes many forms; religious devotion in worshipping God to whom we owe everything we have, patriotism in honoring our country that makes our life possible, obedience to authority which cares for the common good, truth to others who have a right to trust us, the justice of punishing appropriately those who do wrong to deter others and maintain public standards, mercy in helping others even when undeserving, affability which we owe to all we meet, and fairness in living, not just by the letter of the law but in view of people's true needs.

But we cannot respect other people's rights nor find the balance of moderation in other matters without prudence, the right use of our intelligence to form our conscience and act on it in the unique situations of our lives. The prudence required to manage one's own life well, is not the same as the prudence that a man as father and a woman as mother need to care for their family, nor the same as the prudence required of persons who manage corporations and governments. The spiritual director of individuals, of parents, of public and professional officials must especially help them to acquire the habits of reflection, foresight, care, creativity, etc., which are required to fulfill their responsibilities in ways that are at once wise and responsible.

Vocations

God has called each person to perform some particular service within the Christian community and the secular society. Until a person has discovered a vocation appropriate to her or his gifts and situation in life, it is difficult to advance spiritually in a consistent manner. The spiritual journey for each of us is not simply our own pursuit of happiness, but a journey with others whom we must assist on the way if we are to be in turn assisted by them. We travel over the seas of life in one boat together and each of us must fulfill his or her proper task if the boat is not to founder.

I have already pointed out that one's special vocation in life, because it is a qualification of the very goal to which we are traveling, a specification of our own proper road to that goal, involves the deepest level of our personality, the level of first principles of action, of insight, and fundamental commitment. Decisions at this level are hidden from the light of ordinary practical life, and are difficult to put into words. This is the area of human life which most properly pertains to spiritual direction. Hence the director must be especially concerned with the problem of vocation or "state in life" and must ask: *What is the vocation from God for this follower of Christ? How is he or she to be fully conscious of it and become firmly committed to it?*

Most people have a vocation to family life that arises from the process we call "falling in love." They feel the need of a human companion for this earthly life, and desire to leave children behind them. This is part of human nature and according to Aquinas if there had been no sin, all human beings would have found a partner and lived a family life, learning through it that unselfish love which would have opened their hearts to God and the community which is God's kingdom for all eternity. The vocation to marriage is thus a life pertaining to this world yet looking beyond it to eternal life.

It is essential, of course, that a spiritual director help a client in choosing a marriage partner, since here the possibility of tragic mistakes is very acute. The principal problem for the Christian must go beyond physical attraction to love of the partner's true character and a sharing of common interests, especially a common faith if that can be achieved. The married have many trials in life, in adjusting and remaining true to each other, in fulfilling their responsibilities to their families. Our society does not provide a very clear vision of what the roles of a father and a mother are, or what true love between man and woman is. The spiritual director must help the couple learn all these things. In particular it is necessary in our society to teach the couple to use their sexual relationships as a means of showing unselfish love and not for the mere pursuit of selfish pleasure, and must teach them the role of self-control and abstinence in marriage both as a means of responsible parenthood, but also as a means of detachment that keeps before their minds that the pleasures of this earth are passing and only the joy of the spirit is enduring.

Yet domestic life does not exhaust the responsibilities of adults. They should never neglect the care of their families, but provided they fulfill this responsibility, their vocation also calls them to a service of the wider community in the various occupations which the community needs. On the one hand the purpose of these jobs is the support of the worker's family, but on the other it is a service to society. The balance between these is not easy, and requires guidance from the spiritual director. Today the ethics of the different professions is full of problems and controversies; so that in guiding professionals, the director must call attention to the ethical aspects of his client's work. The teacher, the lawyer, the physician, the businessman cannot advance in genuine holiness except through the special services they provide.

In our world, however, the church is a community of witness, a leaven within the secular society, to which every Christian ought to make their contribution, not merely of money, but also of time and talent. First of all the Christian community calls some of its male members to serve the community as its sacred ministers of the sacraments and doctrinal preaching and teaching, and they are empowered by the sacrament of ordination to do this task not simply in the name of the community they serve, but in the name of God and his Christ. They act *in persona Christi.* God also calls some female members to serve the community in prayer and penance in consecration as brides of Christ to keep before the mind of all Christians the eschatological goal of life, the heavenly wedding feast. Without them the Christian community will bear little fruit, while through their prayers, as through the prayers of Mary and the holy women at Pentecost (Acts 1:14) the Holy Spirit will descend upon it in renewing life.

These two vocations for men and women in the service of the Christian community make little sense to our secular society, and God's call which must go out to many of the baptized, is stifled in the lives of many by the falsehoods of the world. It is a special task of the spiritual director to detect signs of such vocation in clients, to awaken them to these signs, enable them to grow as they commit themselves to God's call. Yet the director should be sure to leave the person free to answer this call, since God gives it in freedom.

The laity, however, while pursuing their own vocation of marriage and of earthly service to the community, have an obligation to share in the work of the church, to foster vocations to the ordained ministry and consecrated life, and yet to give to the world that witness of justice and charity which they as sharers in the life of the world can most effectively give—the lay apostolate. Directors should never see their task as simply helping individuals to personal holiness apart from the service of the church and the world, that would be a false holiness.

The Sacraments of Confirmation, Marriage, Holy Orders

Certain of the sacraments are directed specifically to assist Christians in this illuminative process in relation to their particular vocations of service in the church. Spiritual directors must ask themselves: *Has my client realized the responsibilities of confirmation common to all Christians? If my client has a vocation to priesthood, does he understand the meaning of holy orders? If my client has a vocation to the reli-*

*gious life, and especially if she has a vocation to the consecrated, con-
templative life, is she aware of what this calling means? Are each of
these responding to this calling in true freedom, or under some illusion?*

Confirmation, which in the Eastern church was given with baptism,
but in the Western church is separated from it when this baptism is not
conferred on adults but infants, expresses the social, ministerial aspect
of baptism and is common to all Christians. As we have said all
Christians once incorporated in the membership of the church incur a
responsibility to serve the church and participate in its ministry to the
world. For this they require the fullness of the gifts of the Spirit which
are given in baptism but, as it were, activated in confirmation.

Within the church, as already explained, there are fundamentally the
two vocations, one to marriage and participation in this earthly life, the
other to witness to the life to come. Jesus prayed to the Father for his
disciples, "I do not ask you to take them out of the world but to keep
them from the evil one" (Jn 17:15). These are the complementary poles
of the Christian life which were realized in Jesus and Mary who lived
the domesticity of home and work, but then left home to pursue the
journey to the cross and resurrection. They are complementary since,
without the Christian family, there would be no church and without
priests and consecrated virgins the church would forget its role and be
dissolved into the world. To these vocations correspond the sacrament
of marriage and of holy orders.

But why is there no sacrament for the consecrated virgin? The
answer seems to be that while marriage belongs wholly to this world,
and priestly ministry, although it points to heaven, is still a ministry of
earth, the role of the consecrated virgin and of all whole life the contemplative life is already an anticipation of heaven, and "sacrament," a
sacred sign in itself.

The spiritual director of priests and consecrated persons, men and
women, and especially of brides of Christ in the contemplative life
have an especially intense task. In the past most spiritual writing was
directed to such persons in whom it is most likely that the higher gifts
of the unitive life will flower. For that reason more will be said about
this task in the next and final chapter.

Chapter 7

The Process of Union

The Theological Virtues

The acquired and infused intellectual and moral virtues relate primarily to how we deal with the created means necessary for us to reach our uncreated goal, while the theological virtues unite us directly to the goal, God in three Persons. Hence, it is obvious that as the moral virtues relate primarily to the illuminative process, the theological virtues relate primarily to the unitive process. Therefore, in seeking to find how closely those we direct are united to God, the question to ask is: *How strong is the faith, the hope, the love of God and neighbor in the one I am counseling?*

It is essential in asking this question to understand that the terms "faith, hope, love" are very ambiguous. Today we speak of the "faiths" of the different religions, and we rightly speak of our "faith" in a trustworthy person. We also "hope" for all sorts of things, and "love" can mean anything from "I love to drink" to "I love my wife and children." The faith, hope, and charity which St. Paul preached (1 Cor 13:13; Rm 5:1–2, etc.), and which we are discussing here are virtues given us by God to enable us to hear and believe what God says, to rely infallibly on his promises of eternal life, and to love God and our neighbor and ourself for God's sake, i.e., to work so that my neighbors and myself will live with God forever. The director must carefully distinguish the signs of truly authentic supernatural faith, hope, and love from all their counterfeits, and especially from hypocritical, superficial, or neurotic imitations.

Faith is the foundation of the Christian life. It is a virtue by which the human intelligence is so transformed that it is capable of recognizing the voice of God speaking through the prophets, the church, the scriptures and ultimately through Jesus Christ and his Holy Spirit. It believes the word of God on the word of God and rests on no other authority. It is given the child in baptism and to the adult in a conversion which baptism completes. Yet although faith transcends reason, it is reasonable, because, though its formal motive is solely the word of God, yet its material conditions are the signs which God has given to make it humanly credible. These signs are both objective and subjective. The objective signs are the fulfillment of prophecies and miracles and the sign accessible to all is the moral miracle of the church. The subjective signs are the gospel's fulfillment of our deepest spiritual needs.[66]

The director seeks to help the Christian achieve a faith that is firm and pure. Such a faith is not blind or uncritical: rather, it is critical in the truest sense of the word; it discerns what is the word of God from lesser truths: what is revealed from what is mere theological speculation or human opinion (especially one's own opinions about what is revealed). Since it is the college of bishops under the headship of the successor of St. Peter, who have alone been given by Jesus the authority to speak in his name in making definitive judgments as to what has been revealed by him, a true Catholic faith accepts without dissent the judgments of this teaching authority, believing on faith what they declare to be of faith, and accepting with religious obedience of mind and will what they teach with lesser definitiveness, giving to it the value assigned by that authority.

The director must help Christians rid themselves of any tendencies either to attribute to any teaching of the church a degree of authority which is not proper to it, or, on the other hand, to elevate personal, theological, or popular opinions to an authority equal to that of the church. A faith that is not conformed to the teaching of the church which is empowered to speak in God's name is no safe guide to God.

Hope is an oft-neglected virtue, but without it faith loses all its vitality. Faith looks toward the unseen goal of life, while hope perceives that goal as really attainable. Luther was saved from despair because he believed that his faith guaranteed him the salvation which he realized his works could not merit. While faith assures us that God wills the salvation of all, it does not reveal who will in fact be saved, and therefore cannot give the assurance which Luther sought. Your name may be written in the Book of Life, but it is not written in the Bible.

But, praise God!, hope does give that assurance, not by revealing which ones of us will in fact be saved, but by telling us that nothing can stand in the way of our salvation, not even our own unworthiness, if we put our trust in God, not ourselves, our works, or any other creature. Hope, therefore, does not presume on God's goodness by neglecting to obey him, nor does it ever despair of his power to save us to the very last moment of our life, but it constantly encourages us to keep striving to do his will with the confidence that he will make our efforts ultimately successful.

Love (*agape, caritas*) is not just any kind of love. It is the love God has for us returned to God and overflowing to all God's creatures—ourselves, our neighbors, all humankind. It is not easy for us in this life, indeed impossible, for us to discern with certitude that this love is genuine and not counterfeited by self-love, yet the sincere reception of the sacraments constantly pours that love into our hearts from the sacred heart itself. This holy love includes, not excludes genuine self-love, love for ourselves for God's sake as we live in his image. Hence, it is always necessary for us to pray to God that he will transform our hearts, that we may love him and his creatures with his own love and nothing less. St. Catherine tells us that the best sign that persons are living in grace is that they serve God in their neighbor, but note that she does not merely say "serve the neighbor" but "serve God in the neighbor."[67]

In St. Paul's heavenly hymn to love in 1 Corinthians 13 we learn that it is this love which informs all the other virtues making them truly Christlike and uniting us to God in total fulfillment of all his laws, but that without it we are not spiritually alive.

The Gifts of the Holy Spirit

A special mark of the Dominican tradition of spirituality is its interest in the role of the gifts of the Holy Spirit. A director in this tradition will be especially concerned to ask: *Are the Gifts of the Holy Spirit fully active in the life of this person? How are they manifested?* Ambroise Gardeil, O.P., in a fascinating work, *The Gifts of the Holy Spirit in the Lives of the Dominican Saints*,[68] has shown how different saints of the order typify the working of each of these gifts in remarkable ways.

This special interest in the gifts is already manifest in the earliest period of the life of the order in Guillaume Peyraut's *Summa of Virtues and Vices*, and in Etienne de Bourbon's vast work on preaching which is organized on the basis of these gifts. St. Thomas Aquinas gave much attention to the question and there is a marked development in his thought from his treatment of the gifts in the *Commentary on the Sentences of Peter Lombard*, to that in the *Summa Theologiae*. His mature view was that these gifts do not transcend the theological virtues of faith, hope and charity, since these directly relate to God and are the consummation of our union with God, but that they are given in order to make the theological and cardinal virtues flexible to the guidance of the Holy Spirit. The reason he gives is that since the goal of our spiritual journey is nothing less than participation in the very life of God, our actions must be proportioned not simply to our human nature and its human mode of behavior but to the mode which God's has in his own life, a divine mode known only to the Holy Spirit and which he alone can inspire. As Jean Poinsot (John of St. Thomas) says,[69]

> From love and union with God, therefore, wisdom and loving and mystical knowledge are derived. By them the intellect is illuminated to judge of divine and created things from an experiential knowledge of God and internal taste of Him, in which charity touches God primarily and creatures secondarily. Hence the same source can enlighten and perfect the intellect in a practical way concerning actions.

Since these gifts are bestowed on all Christians in baptism, it follows, as the Ven. Juan Arintero and Reginald Garrigou-Lagrange argued, that all Christians are called to exercise these gifts in their fullest.[70] They have shown that it was the teaching of St. Thomas Aquinas that until these gifts are fully actualized no Christian can be fully prepared in holiness to enter the beatific vision immediately at death.

As we have already seen, four of the gifts correlate with the four cardinal virtues: the gift of fear of the Lord with temperance, fortitude with fortitude, piety with justice, counsel with prudence; while the other three correlate with the intellectual virtues: faith with insight, hope with science, and love with wisdom. This correlation of the intellectual virtues with the theological virtues makes sense if we remember that: (a) faith is insight into the fundamental truths of the Creed; (b) hope sees a promise of eternity in the temporal things which science studies; (b) love is the dynamism of our whole moral life which culminates in divine wisdom, the threshold of the beatific vision.

These correlations, therefore, indicate how the gifts give a divine mode to the actions of the virtues. Thus, as Gardeil shows, the gift of fear of the Lord gave to the chastity of a St. Louis Beltrán, Rose of Lima, or St. Agnes an instinctive aversion to all impurity and an absolute fidelity to Christ; the gift of fortitude gave to St. Peter Martyr and St. John of Gorcum an unflinching fearlessness in the face of death; the gift of piety to Savonarola or Bartolomé de las Casas a surety of prophetic witness to justice; the counsel of St. Raymund of Peñafort or St. Antoninus a great practicality of prudence; the insight of St. Catherine a profound grasp of the articles of faith, the science of St. Dominic or St. Albert the Great a compassionate understanding of the needs of ignorant humanity, and the wisdom of St. Thomas Aquinas a burning love of the truth which is God.

Infused Contemplation and Mysticism

A spiritual director finds that nothing seems so significant in the inner lives of those he counsels as certain insights they receive in prayer that lead them on to a new plane of the Christian life. These insights are ordinarily not "visions" or "revelations" (although in the Middle Ages they might have been described as such), but simply new and deeper understandings of the truths which the persons have heard preached all their lives and have sincerely believed, but never before understood very well, and which now seem to become transparent and strike deep in their hearts so that they can turn to God in a new trust and love. The director ought to ask: *Are these insights which seem to be deepening the spiritual life of this person truly the action of the Holy Spirit's Gifts?*

When such experiences prove genuine by the fact that they conform the person's mind to the word of God as taught by the church in accordance with scripture and tradition and when they purify the person's motivations and result in the fruits of good works, the director can reasonably attribute them to the Holy Spirit and to the operation of his gifts. Such events occur, I believe, in every Christian who practices the virtues, frequents the sacraments, and is constant in prayer, often in the fervent reception of holy communion, and they are part of the process of union, the more and more intimate commitment to God which anticipates the goal of the Christian journey.

This union is effected through the acts of the theological virtues of faith, hope, and love. According to St. Thomas the image of God by which we are assimilated to him is perfected in these acts and this union constitutes the "indwelling of the Trinity" by which God is in the soul as in his temple, as the glory of God, the Shekinah, was in the Holy of Holies of the tabernacle in the desert (Ex 40:34–35) and the Temple at Jerusalem (1 Kgs 8:10–11). It is a presence of God which is the dawning of eternal life, an absolute contact with God which is the same as the union with him in heaven, except that it still takes place in the night of faith, rather than in the daylight of vision.

No earthly vision or revelation or miraculous phenomenon can bring the soul closer to God than such simple acts of faith, hope, and love which every Christian by baptism is able to perform. It is essential, therefore, for directors to make it clear to Christians that the earthly goal of the spiritual journey is not some extraordinary experience, but simply union with God by profound acts of faith, hope, and love. This teaching of Aquinas is affirmed by all the great spiritual doctors of the church, not only by the Dominican St. Catherine, but by the Carmelites St. John of the Cross and St. Teresa of Avila. True prayer must become second nature so that we often do not realize we are truly praying. The down-to-earth Fr. Vincent McNabb of the English Province said,[71]

> If you and I took these two parables [Lk 18; the Importunate Widow, and the Publican and the Pharisee] to heart and lived them, we should know how to pray, even though we might not know we knew. The publican did not know he was justified. If you had asked him, "Can you pray?" he would have said, "No, I cannot pray. I was thinking of asking the Pharisee. He seems to know all about it. I could only say I was a sinner. My past is dreadful, I cannot imagine myself praying. I am better at stealing."

What then is "mystical prayer" or "infused contemplation"? Again it was Arintero and Garrigou-Lagrange who demonstrated from the theological principles of Aquinas and from the experiences of the saints that this highest form of prayer is simply the result of the full operation of the gifts of the Holy Spirit, especially the intellectual gifts of insight, science, and wisdom, giving to the acts of theological virtues their fully divine mode. For example, someone who has all her life meditated on the truths of the faith, experiences now that her acts of faith have become inspired by the Holy Spirit in such a way that they carry her beyond any effort of her own deep into the light of God to an understanding that is beyond all human expression. As St. Catherine of Siena cried out:[72]

> And what shall I say? I will stutter, "A—a," because there is nothing else I know how to say. Finite language cannot express the emotion of the soul who longs for you infinitely. I think I could echo Paul's words: The tongue cannot speak nor the ear hear nor the eye see nor the heart imagine what I have seen! What have you seen? "I have seen the hidden things of God!" And—what do I say? I have nothing to add from these clumsy emotions [of mine]. I say only, my soul, that I have tasted and seen the abyss of supreme eternal providence.

This experience seems to be what Meister Eckhart was trying to express in very different terms, as the birth of the Son of God by the power of the Holy Spirit in souls that have been emptied of all creaturely desires and notions:[73]

> All holiness is from the Holy Spirit. Nature does not overstep her bounds; she always begins working in the lowest and so works up to the highest. The masters say that air can never turn into fire unless it has first become subtle and hot. The Holy Spirit takes the soul and purifies it in light and grace, drawing it up into the all Highest. Hence He says: "In the consecrated place I shall likewise rest." God rests in the soul to the same extent as the soul rests in God. If it rests in Him in part only, He rests in it in part. If it rests completely in Him, He rests completely in it. Hence Eternal Wisdom says: "I shall likewise rest...." Being is the Father, unity is the Son with the Father, goodness is the Holy Spirit. The Holy Spirit receives the soul, the consecrated place, in its clearest and highest form, and carries it up to His origin, that is the Son, and the son carries it further to His Origin, that is the Father, into the ground, the beginning where the Son has His being. There eternal Wisdom likewise rests in the consecrated and holy city, in the innermost place....Whenever the Word speaks into the soul and the soul answers in the living Word, the Son begins to live in the soul....For like operates strongly on like. Hence the soul should

arise in her natural light into that which is highest and clearest, and thus enter into angelic light, and with the angelic light pass into Divine Light, and thus dwell between the three lights as the cross-roads above, where the lights meet. There eternal life speaks life into her, there the soul becomes alive and speaks again in the Word.

These experienced mystic writers say that it is the beginning of this infused contemplation or regular action of the Holy Spirit in guiding the soul through his gifts that is the cause of the detachment of the soul from merely sensitive life in the dark night of the Soul which marks the transition to the illuminative phase of the spiritual journey and which steadily increases if the illuminative phase is consistently lived through. Finally, as it comes to predominance in the maturing soul, the Christian passes from the illuminative phase to the unitive and to full Christian maturity through the dark night of the Spirit.

This night of the Spirit consists in the purification of the theological virtues by the full action of the intellectual gifts of the Spirit. It reaches to the very depths of the soul and burns out the last traces of the effects of original and personal sin. Because it reaches to the very core of the person it entails a suffering like that of Christ on the cross who called out "My God, my God why have you abandoned me!" Only as the soul approaches very close to perfect union with God does it finally come to see how far away from him it is as a creature and vastly further as a sinner.

Spiritual writers, and especially Dominican ones, who are convinced that all Christians are called to infused contemplation, puzzle over the fact that even some very holy persons do not seem to experience this mystical prayer. Garrigou-Lagrange explained this evident difficulty by noting that some great saints, like St. Vincent de Paul, who engage in a very intense active ministry simply do not have the peace and quiet necessary to enter fully into the contemplative life. Although in them the theological virtues, and especially that of charity, are wonderfully advanced, yet the intellectual gifts of the Spirit are still operating only obscurely. Consequently, Garrigou-Lagrange believed that for such active saints this final purification and infused contemplation are delayed until the last days of life when, in correspondence to the high degree of their charity, it takes effect very rapidly so as to be complete at death.

Granted that this may well be the case, one should recall that God said to St. Catherine not to judge all souls by her own experience because God deals with each soul in unique ways. We are speaking of the action of grace, which no one can claim to have merited by their life, no matter how holy. Hence no one ought to judge that their lack of this gift of infused contemplation is due to any lack of love for them on God's part, nor necessarily the result of any fault of their own (although it may well be), but rather to continue on their journey, content to let God guide and purify them as he sees best. [74]

Perhaps it is the case that this gift of infused contemplation is far more common than we imagine—that at least moments of such deepened insight and love take place in the lives of all sincere Christians and throughout their lives, but in such quiet and undramatic ways that they are not recognized, so that in some souls this purifying and illuminating and uniting action of the Holy Spirit becomes constant while remaining obscure. Naturally, it is only in the lives of the great saints, who have lived the Christian life with such great intensity that their sanctity has become visible as a witness to others, that this mystical prayer takes on a dramatic, phenomenal character. Every Christian can and should pray for the fulfillment of these gifts of the Spirit, but should not be concerned to enjoy them experientially, but instead to believe, hope in, and love God with a whole heart. As the early Dominican Guillaume de Peyraut (d. 1271) wrote:[75]

> Birds when they fly spread their wings. So should we spread the wings of our heart in yearning and wait always for the hour of revelation, so that at whatever hour the breath of divine inspiration dissipates the clouds of our mind, our soul will unfold its wings of contemplation and will lift itself and soar aloft with its gaze fixed on that light of eternity which streams from above. Thus it will fly above the clouds of worldly vanity.

And in the seventeenth century Alexander Piny, O.P., spoke of the "prayer of the heart" which he did not claim to be mystical but still very fruitful:[76]

> Prayer is nothing else than a raising or loving union of the soul with God, or, at least having that loving union as its principal goal....It is easy therefore to see what is meant by "the prayer of

the heart."...[It] is nothing else but a loving union of our will with God...during the entire time of that prayer. Thus one makes this prayer perfectly as long as the soul remains disposed to will to continue to love, adore, and pray to God.

Mystical Espousals and Marriage

The symbolism of the spiritual union of the human person with God as a "marriage" is perfectly biblical. The prophets portray the covenant between Yahweh and Israel as a marriage in which there is fidelity or infidelity on the part of Israel but not on the part of Yahweh who is always faithful.[77] Traditionally, even among the rabbis, the Song of Songs was (and still is by some exegetes[78]) read as an allegory of this mutual love of God and Israel, or perhaps of the Messiah and Israel. In the New Testament, Jesus refers to himself as the Bridegroom (Mt 9:15, 25:1, 6; Mk 20:19; Lk 5:34; Jn 3:29) and the kingdom of Heaven as a wedding banquet; 2 Corinthians 11:2; Ephesians 5:23 speak of Christ as the bride of his church, and the same metaphor is used in Revelation 19:7, 9; 21:2, 9:22:17. No wonder then that Christian mystics have adopted the same symbolism.

Note that it applies to every Christian as a member of the church who enters into the covenant of love with God at baptism, When the mystics use it, therefore, they are only recognizing that this baptismal covenant is consummated in heaven and anticipated, as it were, at the completion of earthly life. While it is a symbolism which is more appropriate for the relation of women to Christ, it pertains to male Christians also in that it expresses the intimacy of friendship.

As a special phenomenon recounted by many mystics, especially women mystics, it is an experience of infused contemplation in which the soul becomes so conscious of Christ's love and its commitment to him that it understands profoundly what St. Paul says:

> I am convinced that neither death, nor life, nor angels, nor principalities, nor present things, nor future things, nor powers, nor height, nor depth, nor any other creature will be able to separate us from the love of God in Christ Jesus our Lord (Rm 5:38–39).

To some mystics it has even been revealed that they are "confirmed in grace," i.e., that they are predestined. Before this actual experience of final union with Christ there may be an experience referred to as an engagement or espousal anticipating the actual spiritual marriage.

The spiritual director who finds that a client is beginning to report difficulty in prayer and an inclination to occupy the time of prayer not with deliberate meditations but simply with acts of faith, hope, or love should suspect that this is a sign of the transition from the purgative to the illuminative way. As long as the person seems to be making progress in the virtues this is a normal development of the illuminative way, and the client should be allowed to follow the prompting of the Holy Spirit and not required to return to praying in the manner of beginners, except when this is natural and easy for them, or necessary in order to pray at all. Nevertheless, such persons should persevere in prayer and should not cease to meditate, especially on the humanity of Christ and his passion and to make acts of penitence, faith, hope, and love insofar as this is possible for them. John Tauler warns us against the error of quietism, which understands contemplation as mere emptiness of mind:[79]

> We must beware of thinking that once persons have reached this point [of mystical union] they can now leave their lower faculties lying idle, and that they have nothing further to do with them except to let them sleep. If they do this, the whole thing will come to nothing. It is essential to go on exercising our lower faculties in the way appropriate to them. Otherwise the Holy Spirit will abandon us, leave us a prey to spiritual pride, rebellion against discipline and intellectual vanity. What we must do is submit ourselves to God's will with greater humility.

When persons who have become mature in virtue and constant in the fulfillment of their obligations begin to enter into what appears to be profound inner trials that may be the dark night of the Spirit, the director should reassure and encourage them to abide in patience and to continue to pray as best they can and if this takes the form of experiences that resemble spiritual espousal or marriage, the director should explain to them that this is only the normal outcome of the life of grace and that they are to put little value on extraordinary experiences or phenomenon, but continue to be concerned only with the fidelity to Christ through the theological and moral virtues. The Holy Spirit will be their true guide if they continue on this sure way.

In the history of the Dominican order there have been, chiefly among the women, an extraordinary number of those receiving in their bodies the sacred wounds of Christ, but these and other remarkable phenomena are not to be valued in themselves, since they do not constitute sanctity, and can all too easily be used by Satan to confuse the recipient and others as to the true nature of holiness.

The two great dangers of the spiritual life, the Dominican writers assure us, are: (a) a lack of courage and constancy which lead the Christian faced with exterior or interior trials to turn back from the straight path, to cease prayer and the practice of virtue, and to engage in the distractions and even the sins of the world; (b) pride by which one comes to trust one's own holiness rather than the grace of God, to be unwilling to take the lowest place in God's service, to become self-righteous and contemptuous of others less spiritually gifted, to be unwilling to obey God and those God has made his instruments to guide us. Without falling into superstition, one must take account of the fact that the closer one comes to God the more determined and subtle becomes the efforts of Satan to turn the Christian from God. He does this by all sorts of temptations, but especially by temptations to his own diabolic sin of pride. The devil's mark is found especially in his skill in setting not just good against evil, but good against good. By producing misunderstandings and conflicts between the servants of God he divides the church, exhausts the energies of the saints, and causes good persons to destroy themselves. Nothing, therefore, can defeat him except the humility to trust in Christ and his church and not in one's own intelligence or good will.

This explains, too, the great importance of devotion to the Blessed Virgin Mary in the spiritual journey. Mary, as a simple human being who in faith received the incarnation in her womb, quietly walked at her divine Son's side, remained faithful to him at the foot of the cross, and after his resurrection and ascension, remained with the church praying for the coming of the Holy Spirit, is the model of genuine humility, and it is by remaining close to her that one can know one is on the right road. It is true that there are quite a few superstitious persons, fanatics, and spiritual frauds who claim devotion to Mary and attempt to force their forms of devotion to her on others, even with threats. But their lack of true devotion to her is proved precisely by the clamor which they raise and their lack of humility and compassion for others.

The Cross

It must be remembered also, that although in the unitive way the gift of wisdom is joined with the perfection of love, and from these result the most profound joy and peace in the soul, nevertheless, the process of purification is never complete in this life nor the liability to sin wholly removed. In the unitive way there is little left to purify in the saints, but by reason of their intimate union with Christ, these Christians now suffer, not so much for their own purification (Christ and Mary had no need of this for themselves), but for that of the church and the world.

Thus we read how one day in the last year of St. Catherine's life while praying for the church in the old St. Peter's in Rome, she saw and felt the boat of St. Peter, the famous picture by Giotto that she had seen at the entrance of the basilica, descend on her shoulders crushing her to the earth. From that moment on to the hour of her death she experienced the most terrible inner agony of her life as she prayed for the reform of the church and of the Order of Preachers. At the same time this horrible suffering did not take away the joy and peace of union with Christ at the depth of her soul.[80]

Jesus' acceptance of the cross was the supreme act of his acceptance of God's will in trust that it is always a loving will. Dominican spiritual writers always insist that true love of God and neighbor is identical with true conformity to the divine will. This was expressed by Mother St. Dominic of the Cross (Marie-Thérèse Gand, d. 1907), who founded the French Congregation of St. Catherine of Siena, as follows:[81]

Amen! there I find repose, peace, joy, consolation, and strength; my hope, my love and my victory. I shall say it by day, by night, with every beat of my heart, and my last sigh shall be: Amen! Come, Lord Jesus!

It was a teaching of Aquinas, not sufficiently appreciated in current theology, that Christ dying on the cross and suffering for the sins of the whole world, at the same moment continued to behold the face of the Father in the beatific vision. If this seems impossible to theologians it is because they have not taken seriously the experiences of the great mystics whose final sufferings consisted precisely in the confrontation of their intense sorrow for sin and their intense joy in God. Thus the doctrine of the cross and of complete submission to God's will is not contradictory to Christian joy, but is mysteriously joined to it.

The Eucharist and Anointing of the Sick

The eucharist is the supreme sacrament, since in it the risen Lord is present in his very body and blood offering himself for his church and the world, and through it we are joined to him body and soul as his mystical body. At the beginning of these chapters on the processes of purification, illumination, and union, I indicated that in a worthy participation in the eucharist these three processes all are joined and culminate in a bridal union. The celebration of the eucharist is the epitome of the spiritual journey of the Christian, and a spiritual director is in a sense simply one who helps us take part in the eucharist worthily. That is why in the Dominican tradition the eucharist is so central as indicated in Aquinas' hymns for the feast of Corpus Christi and his extensive study of its theology in the *Summa*. Luis de Granada, O.P., the very influential spiritual writer of the seventeenth century said:[82]

> Thus the very reason that caused Jesus to die also made him institute this sacrament [the Eucharist], because, just as love was what brought him from heaven to earth, and made him place himself in the hands of sinners, so it is love which now makes him come once more into the world in this way and which places himself in the same hands. From this it is clear that on his side the cause of this mighty work was none other than his immense love; and from our side, nothing else but our great need. It came out of his mercy alone. Whence it follows that this divine sacrament is the common remedy of the just and sinners, for not only is it the food of the healthy, but also the medicine of the sick. Not only is it the life of the living, but the resurrection of the dead.

In particular, devotion to the eucharist gives to Dominican spirituality its sense of *communio*—that the spiritual journey, although it may seem lonely at times, is in fact the pilgrimage in which we are accompanied by the whole church in mutual support.

Also, the theme of the communion of the saints found in the Apostle's Creed is directly connected with the eucharist in the Dominican tradition. Our prayers for each other help us through this life, but we are also helped by the prayers of those who have gone before us and have reached heaven. Dominican mystics like Mechtilde of Magdebourg express in their revelations this constant sense of the presence of the church triumphant, the blessed saints and angels who are with us invisibly throughout our lives. Our spiritual directors are angels of God to guide us, but not the only ones.

Today the notion of purgatory has become dim in the imagination of many Christians. Like Protestants they suppose that since we are saved by the grace of Christ, the believer must pass straight from earth to heaven. Some have even misinterpreted the liturgical change of Vatican II which eliminated the use of black in the mass for the dead to mean an elimination also of purgatory. Yet the church continues to pray for the dead, why? It becomes clear why, if we remember that our spiritual journey from beginning to the end, no matter how holy we become, continues to involve the work of purification. If we have submitted to this purification totally and unreservedly then no doubt the work of grace will be completed by our death and we will pass immediately to final and eternal union with God. But in actual fact how many walk the way to God with such absolute fidelity?

Consequently, even after death our purgatory, begun long ago here on earth, must still come to its completion, no longer by our own meritorious efforts but by the prayers of the living for whom good works are still possible. We have seen that the deepest purification of the soul is a passive process of submission to the action of God which penetrates the depths of our spirits where we no longer have the wisdom to go. Hence, the souls in purgatory, who are no longer able to do good works, must passively suffer the completion of this divine work. We should pray for the courage to have it finished in us before death!

Yet if we must undergo it, we should not fear it, any more than we should fear purification in this life, because it is a blessed process of healing, however painful, which brings renewed life not death. Dante, who was a Franciscan tertiary, was also a pupil of a pupil of Aquinas, and in his *Purgatorio* he has beautifully described purgatory as a holy place of music, of hope, and of yearning love.

The Holy Spirit

In this book I fear I have not said enough explicitly of the work of the Holy Spirit. The risen Christ sent the Holy Spirit on the church in response to prayers of Mary and the faithful remnant of apostles and holy women to sanctify and animate it. The whole work of sanctification pertains to the Holy Spirit, and the spiritual director is only one of instruments the Spirit uses in this work. Spiritual directors will be successful exactly to the degree that they become sensitive to the work of the Spirit in those they guide and help them to respond to the Spirit's gentle urgings, not simply to the advice of their director. What the director should be trying to do is to get clients to listen to the true voice of the Spirit and not to their own opinions or those of the world. If directors do their work well, the Christian will be able to exclaim as St. Catherine did—she who had such good Dominican directors:[83]

O eternal Trinity, when I received with the light of most holy faith your light you gave me, I came to know therein the way of great perfection, made smooth for me by so many wonderful explanations. Thus I may serve you in the light, not in the dark, and I may be a mirror of a good and holy life; and I may rouse myself from my wretched life in which, always through my own fault, I have served you in darkness. I did not know your truth, and so I did not love it. Why did I not know you? Because I did not see you with the glorious light of holy faith, since the cloud of selfish love darkened the eye of my understanding. Then with your light, eternal Trinity, you dispelled my darkness.

Notes

1. *The Flowing Light of the Godhead,* Lucy Menzies, trans. (London: Longmans Green, 1953, Fifth Part, n.24).
2. Humbert of Romans, *Treatise on Preaching* in Simon Tugwell, *Early Dominicans: Selected Writings,* Classics of Western Spirituality series (New York: Paulist Press, 1982), p. 220.
3. Ibid., pp. 94-103. The *Tractatus de Forma Orandi,* ed. by Albert Wimmer (Ratisbon, 1902), attributed to St. Albert the Great, but probably by Guillaume de Peyraut, Part II, c. 4, has a remarkable treatment of praying with the body based on examples taken from the Bible.
4. P. Régamey, O.P., "Dominican Principles of Spirituality" in Jean Gauthier, et al., *Some Schools of Catholic Spirituality,* translated by Kathryn Sullivan, R.S.C.J. (New York: Desclée, 1959), pp. 76–109, quotes the noted Dominican historian Père Mandonnet (from *France dominicaine,* Feb. 1951, pp. 35–39) as saying "Dominican spirituality is *enlightened, theological, contemplative, individualistic [personalistic], supernatural, apostolic, liturgical, and ascetic*" (p.105). A more recent effort to characterize this spirituality was given by Edward Schillebeeckx, O.P., in an essay, "Dominican Spirituality or the 'Counter Thread' in the Old Religious Story as the Golden Thread in the Dominican Family Story" summarizing an article in *Dominican Topics in South Africa,* March, May, August, 1975 in which he listed these points (a) "faith in the absolute priority of God's grace in human activity;" (b) "religious evangelical living as the atmosphere within which a Dominican is apostolic by proclaiming the Gospel in every possible way," (c) "spirituality directed toward Jesus, especially the humanity of Jesus seen and experienced as a personal

149

manifestation of God for the good of mankind"; (d) "a spirituality which is a 'presence to the world,' which seeks to understand
contemporary times;" (e) a spirituality that acknowledges things
in their own right and only then considers their relation to God;
(f) "a spirituality that explicitly respects the charisms of fellow-
Dominicans with a view to the overall aims of the order"; (g)
other elements that are common to other orders such as Office,
religious observance and community life.

5. Attributed by some to Jean de Montlhéry (13th century), *Libellus
   de instructione novitiorum* in *Opera de vita regulari*, ed. J.J.
   Berthier (Rome, 1889), t. 2, 525–44, appendix.

6. *Lives of the Brethren of the Order of Preachers*, translated by J.
   P. Conway, O.P., edited with notes and introduction by Bede
   Jarrett (London: Burnes Oates/New York: Benziger, 1924,
   reprinted London: Blackfriars Publications, 1955 (Pt. 4, Ch. 1),
   pp. 134–35.

7. Original text *Epistolae encyclicae* in *Opera*, II, 485–524, translation by Bertrand Mahoney, O.P., p. 520

8. W. Van der Marck, O.P., "Geschichte und Ursprung des thoma-
   seides im Dominikanerorden," *Bijdragen: Tijdschrift voor
   Filosofie en Theologie* (vol 1., 26), 1965, pp. 433–443. The oath,
   for which there had been no previous *ordinatio*, was established
   by a *confirmatio* (!) in 1629.

9. Venturino had attempted to lead a great pilgrimage to Rome for
   church reform, but he was a poor organizer and his activities fell
   under censure by the Avignon pope, so that the friar was exiled
   to France for eight years, after which he went with crusaders to
   Smyrna where he died. His works are published in G. Clementi,
   Il b. Venturino da Bergamo. Storia e documenti, 2 vols. (Rome,
   1904).

10. Eckhart, however, was not speaking of an ecstatic but of an habit-
    ual union with God. See Richard Kieckhefer, "Meister Eckhart's
    Conception of Union with God." *Harvard Theological Review*,
    lxxi (1978): 203–225.

11. On this issue in Eckhartian spirituality, see Richard Kieckhefer,
    "The Role of Christ in Tauler's spirituality," *Downside Review*,
    96, n, 324 (July 1978, p. 176–191.

12. Girolamo Savonarola, *Commentary on the Lord's Prayer*, trans-

lated from the Italian by a Dominican Tertiary (Ruth N. Albright), New York, *The Torch Magazine* 33 (1949): Oct., 16–17; Nov. 5–6, 30; Dec. 25–26; 34 (1950), Jan. 23–24; Feb. 13–14, 32; Mar. 13–14, 31; Apr.21–22; May 9–10, 30.

13. *The Lives of the Brethren* also relates the institution of the *Salve* procession in Dominican houses after Compline by Jordan of Saxony c. 1221 and it is also sung at a Dominican death-bed. This beautiful antiphon was probably written in the 11th century by Hermanus Contractus of Reichenau. It was used as a processional chant at the great Benedictine monastery of Cluny as early as c. 1135.

14. Perhaps Dante also confused her with St. Mechtilde of Hackeborn, a younger friend of Mechtilde of Magdebourg.

15. *Essay on the Re-Establishment in France of the Order of Preachers*, edited by Simon Tugwell, O.P., with an introduction by André Duval, O.P., Dominican Sources in English (Parable/Dominican Publications, Dublin, USA, 1983), p.21.

16. *The Intellectual Life*, translated by Mary Ryan (Westminster, MD: Newman Bookshop, 1947), pp. 36–37.

17. Melchior Cano, O.P., *Victory over Self*, translated by Edward J. Schuster, based on Giovanni Battista Carioni da Crema (1530), pp.6–7.

18. *Libro d'amor di carità* (Florence, 1595), folio 144 v.

19. From Sermons 52 and 48, *Meister Eckhart: The Essential Sermons: Commentaries, Treatises and Defense*, translated by Edmund Colledge, O.S.A. and Bernard McGinn, Classics of Western Spirituality (New York: Paulist, 1981) pp. 56 f. and 198.

20. *Summa Theologiae* I, q. 92. The notorious statement of Aristotle that "the female is a misbegotten male" which Aquinas quotes did not mean that the female falls short of being of the same species as the male but that when a male begets a male his action as an efficient cause attains its full term by producing his like, while when he begets a female it does not, because his efficiency in that case does not completely dominate the matter supplied by the female, so that the female influence predominates and the female offspring resembles the female parent rather than the male. It was an attempt at an embryological explanation of a phenomenon which applied to all sexual reproduction among living

things. Unhappily all sorts of unwarranted deductions about human persons were made from it.

21. Venturino de Bergamo, *Tractatus et Epistolae Spirituales*, n. 15, *De remediis contra temptaciones spirituales*, n.4, p. 91, ed. Clementi, see note 9 above.

22. Albert Weiss, O.P., *The Christian Life*, trans by Sister M. Fulgence, O.P., (St. Louis: B. Herder), p. 68.

23. *Commentary on the Gospel According to St. John*, *Opera Omnia*, ed. A. Borgnet (Paris: Vives, 1890–99), vol. 24.

24. *The Prayers of Catherine of Siena*, ed. and trans. Suzanne Noffke, O.P. (New York: Paulist, 1983), Prayer 21, p. 192.

25. For his views see *Surnaturel: études historiques* (Paris: Aubier, 1946) and *A Brief Catechesis on Nature and Grace* (San Francisco: Ignatius Press, 1980). For a Thomistic reply see J.-H. Nicolas, O.P., *Les Profondeurs de la Grace* (Paris: Beauchesne, 1969).

26. Sermon 22 in M. O' C. Walshe, trans. and ed., *Meister Eckhart: Sermons and Treatises* (London: Watkins, 1981), 2 vols. I am indebted for several of my quotes from Eckhart to Judy Schaefer, O.P.

27. Sermon on Passion Sunday, in *Sant'Antonino, O.P. : Maestro di Vita spirituale*, (Florence: Libreria Editrice Fiorentina, 1959), p.134.

28. *Theologia Mentis et Cordis*, X, Dis. III, C. ii, *Reflexio*, p. 196, my translation. Contenson is alluding favorably to a saying of Thomas à Kempis, an author usually considered anti-intellectual.

29. *St. Catherine de Ricci: Selected Letters* Dominican Sources, edited, selected and introduced by Domenico Di Agresti, trans. by Jennifer Petre (Oxford: Dominican Sources, 1985). Letter of 18 Nov, 1549, pp. 14–15.

30. *Pathways of Love*, trans. by a Sister of the Perpetual Rosary (B. Herder, St. Louis), 1959.

31. *L'amour de la Sagesse Eternelle* (Calvaire Montfort, à Pont-Château, 1932), I, nn. 8–12, p. 45. An English translation is available in *God Alone: The Collected Works of St. Louis Mary de Montfort* (Bay Shore, NY: Monfort Publications, 1988), pp.47–122.

32. *Rectitude* (New York: McMullen Books, 1953), p. 232.

33. *De Vita Spirituali ex comentariis B. Hugonis de Sancto Charo, O.P. super totam Bibliam excerpta*, ed. Denis Mézard, O.P. (Ratisbon: F. Pustet, 1910), c. 51, pp. 416–418. My translation.

34. *Tractatus et Epistolae Spirituales*, n. 15, *De remediis contra temptaciones spirituales*, p. 144.

35. *Tractatus de Vita Spirituali*, in *Oeuvres de Saint Vincent Ferrier*, (Paris, 1909), ed. P. Fages, O.P., tom. 1, "That through suitable instruction one may more quickly and easily come to perfection than by oneself," VI, p. 24.

36. John of St. Thomas, *The Gifts of the Holy Ghost*, trans. by Dominic Hughes, O.P. (New York: Sheed and Ward, 1951), Chapter 5, n. 23 pp.168–69.

37. *Victory Over Self*, Chapter 11, p. 152.

38. *Dialogue*, Chapter 97.

39. *The Mystical Evolution*, vol 1, pp. 309–312.

40. *Dialogue*, Chapter 104.

41. *Treatise on the Spiritual Life*, c. 13. Ed. Garanta-Forcada, pp. 513–514, trans. from *The Liturgy of the Hours*, (New York: Catholic Book Publishing Co., 1975), vol. 2, p. 1763.

42. *Dialogue*, Chapter 56.

43. James A. Weisheipl, *Friar Thomas D'Aquino* (Garden City, N.Y.: Doubleday, 1974), p. 235.

44. Matthew Fox, *Original Blessing: A Primer in Creation Centered Spirituality* (Santa Fe: Bear and Co, 1983).

45. Yves Congar, "On the Holy Angels" in *Faith and the Spiritual Life*, trans. by A. Manson and L.C. Sheppard (London: Darton, Longman and Todd), p.12 and p.14.

46. Robert Coles, *The Spiritual Life of Children* (Boston: Houghton Mifflin, 1990).

47. *Theologia Mentis et Cordis* (Paris: Vives, 1875), Tom. 3, Lib. X, Dis iii, C. 1, Reflexio, p. 192. My translation.

48. *Victory Over Self*, Chapter 11, p. 152.

49. *Dialogue*, n.5.

50. Suso, *The Life of the Servant*, trans. by James M. Clark, (London: Faber and Faber, 1952).

51. Sermon 2, Walshe (note 26 above).

52. From Padua, June-July, 1229, in *To Heaven with Diana: A Study of Jordan of Saxony and Diana d'Andalo, with a translation of*

the letters of Jordan by Gerald Vann, O.P. (London: Collins: New York: Pantheon, c. 1960), p. 107.

53. Letter to Dr. Castillo, ed. L. Getino, *La Patrona de America*, (Madrid, 1928), p. 54, trans. from *The Liturgy of the Hours* (New York: Catholic Book Publishing Co., 1975, IV, p. 1342.

54. *Tractatus de Vita Spirituali, Oeuvres de Saint Vincent Ferrier* ed. P. Fages, O.P., (Paris, 1909), tom. 1, p.17, ff. *On silence*, p. 18. He especially praises poverty, silence, and prayer.

55. St. Raymund of Peñafort, Letter, *Monumenta Ord. Praed. Hist* 6, 2 (Rome, 1901), pp. 84–85, in *The Liturgy of the Hours* (Catholic Book Publishing Co., 1975), I, p. 2189.

56. John of the Cross, *The Dark Night of the Soul*, trans. by E. Allison Peers (Garden City, NY: Doubleday-Image Books, 1959), Bk. II, Chapters V-VI, pp. 100–108.

57. Mary Ann Fatula, *Catherine of Siena's Way*, The Way of the Christian Mystics, vol. 4 (Wilmington, DL: Michael Glazier, 1987), p.39.

58. *The House of Gold* (Westminster MD: Newman, reprint 1945) pp.24–25.

59. See my article, "Retirement or Vigil," *Review for Religious* (May, 1972): 325–41.

60. "Declaration on the Relationship of the Church to Non-Christian Religions" (*Nostra Aetate*), Oct. 28, 1965, nn.2–4.

61. *Bede Jarrett Anthology*, ed. by Jordan Auman, O.P. (Dubuque: Priory Press, 1961), pp. 245–47.

62. Vincent of Beauvais, *De eruditione filiorum nobilium*, ed. by Arpad Steiner (Cambridge MA: Medieval Academy of America, 1938) Chapter 12, p. 46.

63. *The Sinners Guide*, trans. by E. C. McEniry, O.P., a new and rev. ed. (Columbus: Ohio: Long's College Book Co. 1946), p. 297.

64. Quoted by Reiner Schürman in *Meister Eckhart: Mystic and Philosopher* (Bloomington and London: Indiana U. Press, 1978), p. 7, from Sermon on the text, "Jesus entered" (Lk 10:38), n.8, p.5.

65. Sermon 5b, Walshe (note 26 above).

66. "The Church herself, with her marvelous propagation, eminent holiness and inexhaustible fruitfulness in everything that is good, with her catholic unity and invincible stability, is a great and per-

petual motive of credibility and an irrefutable testimony of her divine mission." Vatican I, *Dei Filius* 3; DS 3013, quoted in *The Catechism of the Catholic Church*, n. 156 and 812. Vatican II, *Lumen Gentium*, n.8, confirms this description of the church as a visible sign or sacrament demanding our faith.

67. *Dialogue*, Chapters 6–7.
68. (Milwaukee: Bruce, 1937).
69. John of St. Thomas, *The Gifts of the Holy Ghost* (note 36 above), Chapter V, n. 10, p. 100.
70. The issue was first brought to public attention in the modern period by two authors who were not Dominicans, A. Saudreau in *Les degres de la vie spirituelle* (Angers, 1896) in controversy with A. Farges who defended the two-way theory.
71. *The Craft of Prayer* (London: Burns Oates and Wasbourne), p.77.
72. *Dialogue*, Chapter 153.
73. Meister Eckhart, Sermon IX, "*Adolescens, tibi dico, surge*," in James M. Clark, *Meister Eckhart: An Introduction to the Study of His Works with an Anthology of his Sermons* (London: Thomas Nelson, 1957), p. 166–169.
74. See Jean-Hervé Nicolas, O.P., *Contemplation et Vie Contemplative en Christianisme* (Fribourg Suisse, Editions Universitaires; Paris: Editions Beauchesne, 1980, pp.36–47 for an extensive discussion of this question. He nuances Garrigou-Lagrange's views by saying that since the Christian life is intrinsically contemplative, by baptism we are all remotely called to contemplation to be attained in eternal life. But most people's vocations do not provide the ordinary conditions which prepare proximately for infused contemplation. Hence, through no fault of their own they may not be called proximately by the Spirit (who acts with sovereign freedom) to infused contemplation in this life, yet may continue to grow in charity. Infused contemplation prepares for the beatific vision, yet is not continuous with it. Hence those who are holy by reason of advanced charity, may not need to pass through purgatory, even if they have not yet experienced infused contemplation.
75. Gulielmus Peraldus, *De Virtutibus et Vitiis*, I (Lyons: P. Campagnon, 1668), Part 4, ix 434b.
76. Quoted from Henri Bremond, *Histoire litteraire du sentiment religieux en France depuis la fin des guerres de religion jusqu'a*

nos jours, 12 vols. (Paris: Librarie Bloud et Gay, 1926–1938), vol. 8, pp. 78–184 on Piny, quote from p. 150.76.

77. In the Old Testament, God is the husband of his chosen people (Hos 1–3; Is 1:21–26; 50:1; 54:6–7; 62:4–5; Jr 2:2; 3:1, 6–12; Ez 16 and 23. Ps 45 and Sg seem to attribute this title to the Messiah (see next note). In the New Testament, Jesus as Messiah is the bridegroom of the church, Mt 22:1–14; 25:1–13; Eph 5:25–33; 1 Cor 6:15–17; 2 Cor 11:2; Rv 19:9; 21:9.

78. For the history of the interpretation of *The Song* see the commentary of A. Robert and R. Tournay (Paris: Études Biblique, 1963).

79. Sermon 40 for the Monday in passion week. *Spiritual Conferences of John Tauler*, trans. and ed. by Eric Colledge and Sister M. Jane, O.P. (St. Louis: B. Herder Book Co, 1961), p. 212.

80. See note 57 above.

81. *Maxims and Counsels*, p. 96.

82. *Memorial of the Christian Life, Treatise 2*, from Kathleen Pond, ed. and trans. *The Spirit of the Spanish Mystics* (New York: P.J. Kenedy and Sons), pp.70–71.

83. *Dialogue*, final chapter.

Select Bibliography

Arintero, Juan G., O.P., *The Mystical Evolution in the Development and Vitality of the Church*, 2 vols. (St. Louis: B. Herder Book Co, 1949).

———, *Stages in Prayer* (St. Louis, B. Herder, 1957).

———, with Mother Mary Magdalene, C. P., *Towards the Heights of Union with God* (Erlanger, NY.: Passionist Monastery, no date).

Ashley, Benedict M., O.P., "The Beginner at Mental Prayer," *Cross and Crown*, 12 (June, 133–145, reissued as Cross and Crown Reprint, 1960).

———, "The Essence of the Dominican Order and Religious Obedience," *Provincial Newsletter Forum*, 1968, 12 pp.

———, "Religious Orders and Social Involvement," *Catholic Mind* (March, 1971): 29–33.

———, "A Psychological Model with a Spiritual Dimension," *Pastoral Psychology*, (May, 1972): 31–40.

———, "Retirement or Vigil," *Review for Religious* (May, 1972): 325–41.

———, "Models for Dominican Relationships," *Exchange*, Fall, 1976, pp. 5–9.

———, "A Guide to St. Catherine's *Dialogue*", *Cross and Crown*, 29 1977): 237–49.

_____, "Three Strands in the Thought of Eckhart the Scholastic Theologian," *The Thomist*, 42 (April, 1978): 226–239.

_____, "What Do We Pray in the Lord's Prayer?" *Spirituality Today* 31, 2 (July, 1979): 121–136.

_____, "St. Catherine of Siena's Principles of Spiritual Direction," *Spirituality Today*, 33, 1 (March, 1981: pp. 43–52.

_____, "An Integrated View of the Christian Person" in *Technological Powers and the Person* (St. Louis: Pope John Center, 1983), pp. 313–333.

_____, *The Dominicans*, Religious Orders Series, No. 3 (Collegeville, MN: Liturgical Press/Michael Glazier, 1990).

Book of Constitutions and Ordinations of the Order of Friars Preachers, Rule and Fundamental Constitution. English edition (Rome: General Curia of the Order of Preachers, 1984).

Cano, Melchior, *Victory Over Self*, translated by E. J. Schuster, *Cross and Crown* 8 (1956), pp. 121, 141, 340–359.

Catherine de Ricci, St., *Selected Letters*, edited, selected and introduced by Dominico Di Agresti, translated by Jennifer Petrie (Oxford: Dominican Sources in English, 1985).

Catherine of Siena, St., *The Dialogue* (New York: Paulist Press, 1980); *Prayers* (Paulist, 1983), translated and introduced by Suzanne Noffke, O.P. *The Letters* are in the process of publication in several volumes by the same editor, *The Letters of St. Catherine of Siena*, vol. 1 (Binghampton: Medieval and Renaissance Texts and Studies, 1988).

Chardon, Louis, *The Cross of Jesus*, 2 vols (St. Louis: B. Herder, 1973).

Eckhart, *Meister Eckhart: The Essential Sermons, Commentaries, Treatise and Defense*, translated and introduced by Edmund Colledge and Bernard McGinn (New York: Paulist, 1981).

Eckhart, *Meister Eckhart: Sermons and Treatises*, 3 vols., translated by M. O'C. Walshe (London, Watkins, 1979, 1981, and 1985).

Gardeil, Ambroise, *The Gifts of the Holy Ghost in Dominican Saints* (Milwaukee: Bruce, 1937).

Garrigou-Lagrange, Reginald, *Christian Perfection and Contemplation*, translated by Sister Timothea Doyle (St. Louis: Herder, 1939).

————, *The Three Ages of the Interior Life*, 2 vols. trans. by Sister Timothea Doyle (St. Louis: B. Herder, 1948). The fullest theological analysis of spiritual life from a Dominican perspective.

Hinnebusch, William A., "Dominican Spirituality" in *New Catholic Encyclopedia*, pp. 971–974.

Jarrett, Bede, *An Anthology of Bede Jarrett*, ed. by Jordan Aumann (Dubuque, IA: Priory Press, 1961).

Lehner, Francis C., ed., *Saint Dominic: Biographical Documents* (Washington, D.C., Thomist Press, 1964). Best collection of basic documents.

Lippini, P. Pietro, *La Spiritualità Dominicana* (Bologna: Edizioni Studio Domenicano, 1987). Although this recent work is still accessible only in Italian, because of its bibliography it is indispensable.

Louis of Granada, *Summa of the Christian Life*, 3 vols. (St. Louis: Herder, 1954).

Louis-Marie-Grignion de Montfort, St., *True Devotion to the Blessed Virgin*, trans. by Frederick William Faber (New York: P. J. Kenedy and Sons, 1909).

Oechslin, R. L., *Louis of Granada* (St. Louis: B. Herder Book Co., 1962).

Raymund of Capua, O.P., *The Life of St. Catherine of Siena by Raymund of Capua*, trans. by Conlith Kearns, (Wilmington, DE: Michael Glazier, 1980).

Savonarola, Girolamo, *The Compendium of Revelations* in *Apocalyptic Spirituality*, ed. and introduced by Bernard McGinn (New York: Paulist Press, 1979), pp. 192–276.

————, *Commentary on the Lord's Prayer*, translated from the Italian by a Dominican Tertiary (Ruth N. Albright), New York, *The Torch Magazine* 33 (1949): Oct., 16–17; Nov. 5–6, 30; Dec. 25–26; 34 (1950), Jan. 23–24; Feb. 13–14, 32; Mar. 13–14, 31; Apr. 21–22; May 9–10, 30.

The Study of Spirituality, ed. by Cheslyn Jones, Geoffrey Wainwright, Edward Yarnold, S.J. (New York: Oxford University Press, 1986. See especially Simon Tugwell, "The Mendicants," 294–295; "The Dominicans," 296–300; Cyprian Smith and Oliver Davies, "The Rhineland Mystics, pp. 315–320; Max Saint, "Catherine of Siena" pp.311–312; Christopher Bryant, "The Nature of Spiritual Direction: Sacramental Confession, pp. 568–569.

Suso, Henry, *The Exemplar*, 2 vols. (Dubuque, IA: Priory Press, 1962), contains several of Suso's works, including his spiritual biography by a contemporary, Elisabeth Stagel.

————, *The Letters of Henry Suso to His Spiritual Daughters*, trans. by Kathleen Goodman (London: Blackfriars, 1955).

Townsend, Anselm, *Dominican Spirituality* (Milwaukee: Bruce, 1934). A translation of a special number of *La Vie Spirituelle*, IV, Aug., 1921 with a number of interesting points of view.

Tugwell, Simon, ed., *Early Dominicans: Selected Writings*, (The Classics of Western Spirituality, New York: Paulist Press, 1982).

Vicaire, M.-H., *St. Dominic and His Times* (New York: McGraw-Hill, 1964). The standard biography.

Vincent Ferrer, St., *A Treatise on the Spiritual Life*, translated by Julienne Morrell and commented by her (Westminster, MD: Newman Press, 1951).

Weisheipl, James A., *Friar Thomas D'Aquino* (Garden City, N.Y.: Doubleday, 1974). Lists English translations of works.

Woods, Richard, *Eckhart's Way (The Way of Christian Mystics*, vol. 2, Wilmington, DE, Michael Glazier, 1986).

Index of Authors and Subjects